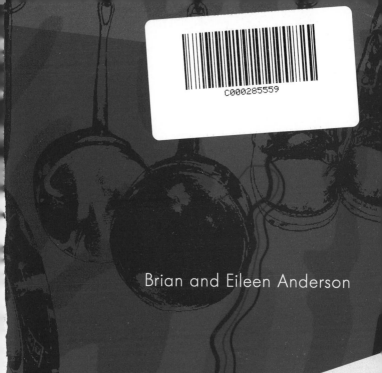

Brian and Eileen Anderson

walk & eat
RHODES

CONTENTS

This pocket guide is designed to add another dimension to a walking holiday on Rhodes. It caters for those who just want to stroll, those who may prefer a longer walk — or even those who are just looking for recommendations on where to eat!

Whether you fly out for a week or a fortnight, you have in your hand enough walks, excursions, tavernas or restaurants and recipes to last throughout — so you can choose the most appealing.

The highlights at a glance:

- 12 varied day walks, each with topographical map or plan
- 2 excursions — one on Rhodes and one exploring a different Greek island
- recommended cafés, tavernas, restaurants and hotels
- recipes to make at your self-catering base or back home
- advice for those on special diets and for wheat-, gluten- and dairy-free eating and shopping on the island

INTRO

THE WALKS

Rhodes is a surprisingly large island, with tourism generally settled around the coastal regions. Apart from exploring the old medieval town of Rhodes, the walks in this book have been chosen mainly to visit well-known beauty spots or the island's spectacular countryside regions — places most tourists never see. Most walks can be reached by bus; for the others (all circular) you will need to use a hire car or taxi.

The walks are of varying distance and range from easy to moderate. The interior of the island is hilly to mountainous, so the *character* of the walks varies considerably. The walk *gradings* in this book all assume comfortable walking conditions, so please remember that while the uphill sections mostly cause no problems for fairly active people when temperatures are comfortable, they can be much more stressful when temperatures rise towards summer heat.

THE EXCURSIONS

Two 'days out' are described. The first is the spectacular and beautiful village of Líndos, where there is an ancient acropolis to explore, colourful and crowded narrow shopping streets to browse, and a beach waiting for you when relaxing becomes a priority. There is a huge selection of places to eat here; we have highlighted one or two. If you prefer a walk before lunch, Walk 11 starts and finishes in Líndos, while Walk 8 ends here.

The second excursion is to the little-known and most easterly of all Greece's islands, Kastellórizo. It's reached by fast catamaran, leaving a good five hours for exploration. The atmospheric harbour itself might be enough to captivate most visitors, but we feature a short walk incorporating a castle, viewpoints, churches and a grain mill. And, of course, there is a restaurant suggestion where you can enjoy good, genuine Greek food.

THE RESTAURANTS AND TAVERNAS

There are hundreds if not thousands of restaurants and tavernas on Rhodes. Many simply serve the needs of a passing trade without ever striving for customer loyalty. Some restaurants turn away from their cultural roots to offer an 'international cuisine'. This generally means that you can enjoy familiar dishes you might find at home, like peppered steaks or chicken Kiev. Many visitors enjoy this type of food, but there is no place for it in this book. All, or at least many of

Other excursions

A number of other Greek islands can be visited from Rhodes. **Sími** is relatively close, and the trip there is a long-standing favourite. The main harbour town stacks up the hillside, one house on top of another, in a most breathtaking fashion. It's a highly recommended trip for those who haven't had the opportunity to visit before.

The introduction of faster catamarans has brought more islands within the reach of day trips, for instance **Tínos, Nísyros, Kos, Kálymnos, Léros**; you could even go to **Marmaris in Turkey**.

Although **Hálki** is nearby, it is not very suitable for a day trip, since the ferry departs late afternoon — except on Sundays, when one leaves early in the morning from *Kámiros Skála* and returns late the same afternoon. Check current times at the Tourist Office.

the restaurants *(estiatório)* and tavernas we have discounted probably serve excellent food in their style, but we were searching for something quite special — restaurants and tavernas offering a good standard of traditional Greek cuisine, preferably with a focus

Taverna sign, Líndos. Below: papa (Greek priest) enjoying a morning break in Psínthos

on Rhodian influences. The use of fresh ingredients was another guiding principle, and this is something to which the Greeks themselves pay a good deal of attention when they eat out. It's usually a good sign when you see a taverna full of locals!

A taverna is a down-to-earth restaurant. In a restaurant you would expect to find your table set with cutlery and glasses and the staff to be more attentive than may be the case in a taverna.

The restaurant menu, too, might be more extensive and include a selection of international dishes. A taverna offers a more relaxed, laid-back atmosphere.

Normally, you sit at an empty table initially; it might have a tablecloth covered with

7

a plastic sheet, but nothing else. A waiter then appears with a fresh paper cloth and, after your order is placed, a bread basket arrives with knives and forks included within. Wine glasses in tavernas are traditionally small tumblers, but more are converting to small wine glasses. Restaurants are mostly associated with larger towns on the island, whereas tavernas can be found everywhere, and they are *all* you will find in the smaller villages and country areas. *And note,* by the way: while a fish taverna (*psarotavérna*) specialises in fish, it will often have grilled meat on offer.

For each of the featured restaurants and tavernas we generally say why we like them and, in a few cases, include a mini-menu listing specialities and/or exceptional dishes. But unlike other books in this series, we haven't included a great many taverna menus, because they are very similar all round the island.

Price guide

Restaurants and tavernas aren't graded or classified by the tourist authorities as they once were, and are no longer subject to price controls. In spite of this, the prices between the various establishments remain surprisingly similar. In general terms, it's much cheaper eating on Rhodes than at home.

The price guides in this book (€ to €€€) indicate 'very reasonable' to 'fairly pricey'. Remember that this guide relates not to prices at home, but to *prices on Rhodes*. The majority of establishments fall into the 'average' category, indicated by €€. Even so, it's always possible to enjoy a relatively inexpensive meal in a top restaurant by choosing carefully from the menu. There's usually a large choice of inexpensive starter dishes which can easily make up a satisfying meal.

Please be aware that no restaurant or taverna has paid in cash or in kind to be included in this guide.

THE RECIPES

Most of the recipes for Greek dishes are fairly well known, but many chefs tweak recipes, often with the use of herbs and spices, to give their dish a special flavour. Only a few of the restaurants we visited seemed willing to share their recipes, possibly because they are not written down but simply passed down through the family. There was also a language barrier when it came to fine details. Many of these restaurants and tavernas are entirely staffed by family. Even the recipes in Greek cookery books have different recipes for the same dish.

We have guessed at the 'secret' ingredients and made all the recipes at home to our own satisfaction. Remember, when you're dining by the edge of the sea, listening to the soft music of lapping waves and watching the sun suffusing the sky with hues of orange and purple as it sinks below a wine-dark sea … the food may taste better than it really is!

Unfortunately, self-catering on a hot Greek island like Rhodes usually means basic equipment — enough to put a breakfast together, but not enough try out our hot recipes. There are usually only two hot plates — one small, for making Greek coffee, and one large. Not to mention the lack of suitable utensils. You'd have to find yourself in really up-market self-catering accommodation to encounter a full cooker!

One-pan meals, fried squid and fried courgettes *can* easily be made on one plate, however. (By the way, olive oil isn't good for frying at high temperatures; it degrades too quickly. Greeks commonly use a lighter sunflower oil or similar for frying.) Cold dishes, on the other hand, *are* easy to prepare in self-catering. (You can buy ready-cooked chickens in many of the larger supermarkets, too.) After a lunch out, a few cold dishes in the evening are ideal to finish off the day. At least when you're back home, trying out recipes you can't cope with in Greece, we might just be able to help you recapture that moment when the sun sank below the sea!

One quick and easy hot one-pan meal we *do* make in self-catering (and often at home) uses a rice-like pasta, *manéstra*. On Rhodes, this is also known by its Italian name, *orzo*. Look for it in the pasta section on supermarket shelves. It looks just like rice and comes in three sizes, small *(mikró)*, medium *(métrio)* and large *(megálo)*. Greek friends recommend the medium size for general use. Look for *kritharáki métrio* or the Italian *orzo medio,* both names under the *manéstra* umbrella. If you make this at home, however, you'll have to bring packets of pasta home from Greece unless you live near a Greek produce supplier or specialist delicatessen. Below is our basic 'throw together' recipe; experiment with it and come up with your own variations. We prefer *manéstra* to rice, as it absorbs flavours beautifully and is so easy to use. But, naturally, if you need a gluten-free option, it's a good recipe for a *risotto*.

Using 50-75 g of pasta per person, select some pre-cooked diced meats (chicken, turkey, pork, etc) and vegetables suitable for a stir fry (chopped onion, garlic, peppers, courgettes, celery, broccoli florets, frozen peas, whatever). Heat olive oil or sunflower oil in a large frying pan/wok, and gently stir fry the *fresh vegetables* with the pasta briefly. Then dissolve a stock cube or two in 250 ml water and stir into the pan. Add more water if necessary. Cover and simmer for 6 min. Stir and check the water, then add seasoning, herbs, the meat and the frozen peas (if used). Cover, bring back to a simmer, and cook a further 5 min. The pasta should be soft if the dish is ready and the moisture absorbed. Serve on its own or with crusty bread and green salad.

Manéstra

EATING GREEK

Eating out for Greek families is a social occasion. It's a pleasure just to watch them. Family and friends gather around the table, men and women sometimes choosing to segregate themselves, with the children up and down as children are. When the food arrives, it's placed in the centre of the table for all to share. Plate after plate arrives until there's hardly room left. The chatter is long and loud, and the pace of eating is slow. Hot food cooling is of no concern. If it's a festive occasion, impromptu Greek dancing quite often follows.

Visitors, on the other hand, usually order a Greek salad for one person, perhaps a *tzatzíki* for another and so on. But there are so many different dishes and flavours to enjoy, it makes sense to **put all the starters in the middle and share**. If you indicate that you would like to eat this way, the waiter will bring small empty plates for each person. Even with only two

11

of you dining, two or three starters can be tried — but it's even better with four or more people eating. After the starters, it's much more acceptable to order individual main courses, although these can be treated in the same way as *mezédes* (appetizers) and shared. We became so used to sharing when living in Greece that we now often share starters and sweets — even in restaurants at home.

After decades of tourism, many tavernas now appreciate that you may not want every course you order to arrive at the same time. But some, especially in country areas, may *not* understand this, so it is best to order *mezédes* first, then order the rest later — or say *argótera* (later) for main courses, etc.

The Greeks **order certain dishes by weight**, usually lamb, pork chops or *kalamári* — all of which will be ordered by the kilo. A half kilo is usually plenty for two people and can be cheaper than ordering by the portion. Fish almost always appears on the menu priced by the kilo. It sometimes looks very expensive when you see the kilo price, but the fish will be weighed and a portion size is usually 300-400 g. If the fish you have chosen is particularly large, the waiter will weigh it for you and tell you its cost to get your agreement.

On the whole, most tavernas are honest about whether or not their **squid (kalamári)** is fresh (*fresko*) or frozen (*katepsig-meno*). Unfortunately, especially in tourist areas, unscrupulous owners may charge for fresh, at the more expensive price, when you've been given frozen. (We were once almost caught this way but, since we were sure of our ground, we insisted on only paying the price for frozen squid. If you feel unhappy, ask for the complaints book which they must produce by law.) Fresh squid usually comes as one piece, lightly fried and melt-in-the-mouth tender. It can be served in rings, but if it is, they will not be heavily breaded or too uniform. You can ask to see the piece being cooked for you. Frozen squid is often rubbery and comes in fairly uniform, crumbed rings. (We did have excellent frozen squid at the Oasis Taverna in Old Rhodes Town, however, and the proprietor told us it had to be specially cut and frozen properly to be tender.)

Fresh *kalamári* — at the market and cooked (note the large piece). Frozen *kalamári* is shown on page 83.

RHODIAN FOOD

Rhodian food mirrors traditional Greek cuisine, but not necessarily the full spectrum of dishes, and there are a couple of Rhodian specialities not widely found elsewhere. One is *pitaroúdia* (chickpea cakes), similar to potato cakes, but flatter. In fact, chickpeas appear in many island recipes. This is good news for those on gluten-free diets, but always ask if any wheat flour has been added.

Over the many years we've been travelling to Greece and enjoying Greek food, the cuisine has always remained traditional and constant. But the influence of the Naked Chef and other high-profile cookery programmes has spread far and wide. Similar programmes on Greek television are bringing a more progressive influence into the country's cuisine, and traditional dishes are starting to evolve. At the moment this is most noticeable in the salads, which are improving in variety and content.

Herbs and spices are intrinsic elements in Greek cooking, especially oregano, thyme and dill, which are sprinkled on everything grilled. On Rhodes, mint (spearmint) is more favoured, especially for sprinkling on cheese and salads. Cumin and *bakári* (allspice) are the two most frequently used spices.

THE MENU

Life would be simpler if the menu (*katálogos*) in Greece was always set out in the familiar way of starters, main courses and sweets. It sometimes is, but then often further divided or subdivided. Fortunately, menus are usually available in English — although they are not always as helpful as they might be. A number of dishes have no direct equivalent. *Hórta (xórta)*, for

Hórta

example, is a dish variously described as boiled greens or spinach. It's the green leaves of the dandelion family (but not strictly dandelions), sometimes collected wild, which are boiled, strained, seasoned, amply tossed in olive oil and lemon juice and served as a single vegetable dish. Very good if it's fresh — a great favourite with the Greeks, and one of our favourites too.

Similarly, familiar dishes such as *mousaká* are described in all sorts of ways — 'meat pie with béchamel sauce' is fairly typical.

The **starters** (*orektiká*) make up the most interesting section, and the list should be quite long. Salads are usually listed here, but may appear in their own section; the same is true for cheese dishes. Starters are a boon for vegetarians and vegans and often suitable for those on gluten-free diets, since many are vegetables served as single dishes — for instance giant butter beans (*gígantes),* beetroot cooked with their leaves (*patzária),* fried courgettes (*kolokithákia tiganitá),* fried aubergines (*melitzana tiganitá*) and the already-mentioned *hórta*. There's an interesting array of dips too, from the familiar *taramasaláta* (cod's roe) and *tzatzíki* (yoghourt/cucumber/garlic) to aubergine dip (*melitzanosaláta*) and garlic/mashed potato (*skordaliá*). On Rhodes *skordaliá* is often served to complement other dishes, like beetroot and, traditionally, cod fish. These dips sometimes appear under the salad list. Still more starter treats include chick pea *keftédes (revithokeftédes),* which are one of our favourites and easy to make. There is a similar speciality only found on Rhodes, *pitaroúdia* (see recipe on page 66). Everybody has their own recipe and it may or may not contain chick peas.

Cheese (*tirí*) dishes on the starters list include *féta* sprinkled with herbs and drizzled with olive oil, *saganáki* (fried *féta* — or another cheese), *saganáki sto foúrno* (oven-baked *féta* with tomatoes and peppers, often spicy), grilled *haloúmi* (a dish borrowed from Cyprus, which is popular on Rhodes), *tirosaláta* (a spicy cheese dip), and *tirokeftédes* (cheese croquettes).

Greek **salad** (*horiátiki saláta*) is synonymous with Greek cuisine for most visitors. There is no standard; it depends on the season, but tomato, cucumber and olives are ever-present, topped by a lump of *féta* cheese and often liberally soaked in olive oil and vinegar. Sometimes it can be a meal in itself. It's on every menu and serves as a useful price comparison between tavernas. Very often we prefer just to have a salad of tomato and cucumber *(domáta/angoúri)*. One salad mostly ignored by visitors, but popular with the Greeks, is lettuce salad *(maroúli saláta)*. It doesn't sound very exciting, but is really tasty the way it's prepared (see page 90). Salads are slowly evolving, cherry tomatoes replacing or supplementing the large Mediterranean tomato, rocket leaves and roasted aubergine adding much more variety.

The **main courses** are listed under *entrádes*, grills and/or meat *(kréas)*, or there may be just one list. Normally, under the *entrádes* you can expect to find **Greek specialities** like *mousakás*, *stifádo* (a veal and shallot stew), *kokkinistó* (veal stew with tomatoes) and *giouvétsi* (veal in a clay pot with *manéstra*, the rice-like pasta mentioned on page 10); the **grills** are found in other sections. **Fish** *(psári)* or **seafood** *(thalasiná)* are normally listed separately.

Beef is served in the form of veal *(moskári)* — beef from a milk-weaned yearling animal. Steaks seem to appear on restaurant menus, whereas tavernas stick with chops *(brizóla)* which are large and meaty. Pork chops *(hoiriní brizóla)* and lamb cutlets *(païdákia)* are popular, but these meats are also served on skewers as *souvláki*. Chicken and fish are also sometimes served this way. Goat *(katsíki)* is popular on Rhodes, and is eaten as chops or a roast which, like lamb, can be ordered by the kilo or by the portion *(merída)*.

Poultry is almost invariably chicken *(kotópoulo)*, but turkey *(galópoula)* is found occasionally.

On a visit to a good supermarket or a market, you will see fresh vegetables in abundance, but you are unlikely to see many **vegetables** with your main course — if any. Chips are fairly ubiquitous, but some dishes like squid *(kalamári)* are served without, so you may need to enquire. Chips *(patátes tiganités)* are always available as a side order with your starters or main course. If you just ask for *patátes,* it's generally understood you want *chips.*

On Rhodes it's fairly typical to find **fish restaurants around coastal regions**. Although predominantly serving fish, fish restaurants invariably offer a selection of meat dishes. There is also a distinct **'meat belt'** on Rhodes, which runs down along the **mountain areas**, at places like Émbonas and Apóllona. Here local lamb and goat are specialities — as well as very hearty village sausage.

Desserts are listed under *glyká,* which means 'sweet'. The Greeks have a sweet tooth and love their sweets soaked in syrup and honey. But these sweets are not a major feature of taverna menus and sometimes don't appear at all. Very often the taverna owner will bring complementary fresh fruit, depending on the season. It might be grapes, watermelon or oranges, but one of our favourites is sliced apple dusted with cinnamon and drizzled with honey. Restaurants usually offer a better menu for desserts.

Greek honey sweets

One of the most popular sweets with tourists is yoghurt and honey which may be topped with walnuts (see page 97). It's not really a traditional Greek sweet, but a response to its immense popularity with visitors. Even if not on the menu it can often be rustled up for you, since the taverna is likely to have a stock of thick, strained yoghurt for making *tzatzíki*.

Baklavá, *kataïfi* and *halvá* are amongst the intensely sweet sweets. *Baklavá*, multi-layered filo pastry sandwiching finely chopped almonds or walnuts, rich in butter and soaked in sugar/honey syrup, finds many devotees (125 g = 695 calories). *Kataïfi*, best described as small shredded wheats (actually a pastry), soaked in sugar/honey syrup appeals to the same group of supporters, as does the *halvá*, a brown, sugar-rich sesame seed confection which is poured into a mould to set.

Galaktoboúriko (recipe on page 85) comes in much lower down the calorie scale. It's vanilla custard sandwiched between layers of filo pastry. *Loukoumádes*, batter balls soaked in honey syrup, is another of the dessert offerings.

Coffee (*kafé*) deserves a special mention. At one time, only 'Nes' (short for Nescafé or any instant coffee) was available: strong enough to 'stand up' the proverbial spoon, it was served with a glass of water. Nowadays, water is still often served, but other options such as filter and cappuccino are commonplace. *A word of caution:* Greek Nes (Nescafé) is stronger and more bitter than its UK equivalent, so use it sparingly when you buy it for use at your hotel or in self-catering.

If you do happen to be in an establishment which only serves Nes, and you're not a lover of very strong coffee, ask for it *elafrí*, weak. Another pitfall to watch out for is added sugar. The Greeks normally have sugar in their coffee, which is sometimes added automatically when it's made. As well as *elafrí*, you need to add *horís zákari* (without sugar). You may require your coffee with/without milk *(me/horís gála)*.

Ordering a **Greek coffee** is quite different. Sugar is added during the preparation, so you need to specify *glykó* (sweet), *métrio* (medium) or *skéto* (without sugar). Greek coffee is never served with milk.

Tea *(tsái)* is widely available — even herbal teas — in restaurants and some cafés. But in some older establishments and in country areas, where tea drinkers are more of a rarity, the need for boiling water to make a decent 'cuppa' hasn't quite filtered through. Don't be surprised if your tea arrives lukewarm. *Zestó vrásto neró* (boiling water) and bubbling gestures with your hands might help!

Frappé

In the heat of summer this is a popular drink for Greeks as well as tourists. Easy to make yourself, either in one of the cheap plastic *frappé* shakers (available in supermarkets) or in a jar with a screw cap. For each *frappé*, put a teaspoon of instant coffee in the container, add ice cubes then half water and half milk (fresh milk, the Greek evaporated milk called *Noynoy*, or soya), plus sugar if wanted. Shake vigorously until the coffee has dissolved and it's nice and frothy.

RHODIAN WINES

Vines are grown extensively in the mountainous regions around Émbonas, where there are a number of successful wine producers. Traditional grape varieties like *Athíri* and *Mandilária* have been grown on the island for centuries. *Mandilária*, it's said, was used to make wine drunk by the Knights of St John. These varieties still provide the bulk of wines made, but more international varieties are now being grown, like Cabernet Sauvignon and Grenache.

Athíri makes a very quaffable dry white wine and is widely used. Ílios and Ródos 2400 on the CAIR label both feature this grape, as does Athíri on the Emery label. Red wine drinkers will not be displeased with Chevalier de Rhodes, based on the *Mandilária* grape, from CAIR, or the Rodon Cabernet Sauvignon from Emery.

In spite of the best efforts of the wine producers to promote the leading labels, the bulk wine released for sale as house wine is virtually the same standard. It's so good and so much cheaper that everybody drinks it, and we have yet to have a house wine on Rhodes that disappointed us. The whites are especially good.

House wine is bought by the kilo, which is effectively the same as a litre. It's a hangover from the days when you went along to the shop with your jug to buy wine from the barrel. With four people your first order would be a kilo, but two might start with a half-kilo *(misó kiló)* and take it from there. The wine often comes in a metal jug or, sometimes, a ceramic jug.

Fast food, Greek-style

The Greeks have been in the fast food market longer than anyone can remember. The pattern of their working life has always been (and still is for most) an early start and an early finish. An early start does not leave time for breakfast, and an early finish means there is time for a good lunch, usually between 2 and 3 in the afternoon.

A mid-morning snack replaces breakfast. Since everybody is still working (in theory), it means a quick dash out to get some finger food, something to carry away and eat immediately. *Gíro me pita*, thinly sliced meat cut from a vertical spit and wrapped in pita with fried onions, a piece of tomato and a dash of yoghurt is hugely popular. *Gíro* (**yee**-ro) on Rhodes is made with pork, although lamb and even chicken can be used or be part of a mix. The pork slices are sprinkled with herbs and spices, stacked and cooked on a vertical rotating spit. *Gíro* sometimes appears on tavernas menus as a simple meal served with chips and a touch of *tzatzíki*.

Pies are a great favourite too, especially *tirópita* (cheese), *spanakópita* (spinach, sometimes with cheese and egg) and *kréatopita* (minced meat). All are made with several layers of filo pastry with the appropriate filling. *Spanakópita* (recipe page 137) is our favourite. Mostly they are individual pies but occasionally they may be made in a large tray and cut into slices (especially true of *spanakópita*).

Pizza, in mini size or slices, has made an appearance in the last decade and become a favourite. More traditional is *souvláki*, lumps of meat on a wooden skewer served with a chunk of bread or in a pita parcel like the *gíro*.

If you have time to wait five minutes, you can order *tost* (a toasted ham and cheese on unbuttered bread). You can specify the filling if you just want one or the other — or even a slice of tomato added.

There are pies for the sweet tooth, too: *mílopita* (apple pie) and, another favourite, *bougátza* (vanilla custard pie).

21

RETSINA, OUZO & SOUMA

It's said that resinated wine, or retsína, originated in the days before wine bottles, when wine was stored in jars or skins sealed with pine resin. When bottles came on the scene, the wine without the resin flavour was not universally popular, so retsína was born. It's generally much preferred by the Greeks — but less so on Rhodes, possibly because the quality of the house wines is so good. Provided the wine is only lightly resinated, it can be quite palatable, and the resin stabilises the wine — which gives it consistency. CAIR makes a good, refreshing retsína, but our favourite is Malamátina. Kourtáki is the best-known brand internationally, but this is moderately resinated and not the easiest retsína for the uninitiated to fall in love with at first sip! Often a pale-coloured retsína signifies less resin, making a more palatable drink for first-timers.

Oúzo is a drink for bright sunshine and bonding, Greek-style. This aniseed-flavoured drink is taken with ice and water and, traditionally, a few nibbles. There are still one or two *oúzeri* around, where you can sit with an oúzo and expect some free *mezédes* (*mezés* for short) — a little plate with a piece of cheese perhaps, a chunk of bread, maybe a few cold chips, or anything to hand. But this tradition is now only usual in country villages away from mass tourism.

When we lived on Lesvos some years ago, the locals insisted that Lesvos made the best oúzo in Greece. We put this down to local pride, but since then we have travelled to many other Greek islands and, sure enough, everybody tells us the best oúzo is from Lesvos. Oúzo 12, Mini and Barbayanni are all leading brands.

Soúma (called *tsípouro* on the Greek mainland and *tsikoudiá* on Crete) is an under-the-counter drink elsewhere, but not on Rhodes. It's made from the distillation of grape alcohol, often from small reject grapes, with flavourings added before distillation. Farmers around Siána on Rhodes were granted a licence by the Italians which was never rescinded, so they can make it legally. It's a powerful, colourless spirit drink which tends to lift the top off the head. Can be a good medicine in the mornings if you're feeling slightly lethargic!

PLANNING YOUR VISIT
When to go

Tourism on Rhodes is seasonal. Charter flights normally start towards the end of April and finish towards the end of October. It's easy enough to reach the island out of season or anytime by taking an international flight to Athens and an internal flight to Rhodes — a journey which can usually be achieved in one day.

The best time for walkers is **spring and autumn**. April is the finest month, especially for flower-lovers, but May is good too. The heat starts to build in June and at some point it becomes too hot to enjoy strenuous walks, but some of the easy or short walks remain possible, especially with an early start. July, August and early September are generally too hot for walking unless you are prepared to rise with the sun and walk very, very early in the morning. Walking in the full heat of the sun in this period is risking serious heat exhaustion and is *most definitely*

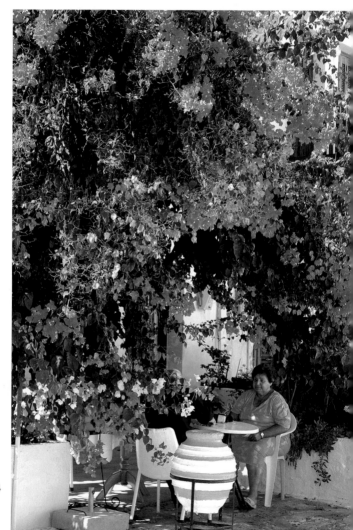

not recommended. Temperatures decline slowly throughout September, and usually by the middle of the month walking is back on the agenda — but it may still be advisable to avoid strenuous walks for a time. By October the temperatures are usually back to the mid or low 20s, and walking becomes a pleasure again.

Eating is a pleasure to be enjoyed anytime of the year so, even if it's too hot to walk, you might still want to try some of our suggested restaurants and tavernas!

Where to stay

There are two clusters of tourist accommodation on the island. The main cluster is around the northern tip, around Rhodes Town, starting at Triánda/Ixiá on the west-facing side of the island and continuing through Rhodes Town down the eastern side through Kalithéa to Faliráki and Kolímbia. The other cluster is around Líndos.

Breezy **Ixiá** catches the prevailing westerlies which pleasantly moderates the heat of summer. It's a resort favoured by many of the island's most luxurious hotels, like the Rodian Beach Amathus (see page 50), which we visit for its excellent Varkarola Taverna. It's well connected by bus to Rhodes Town. **Rhodes Town** has many hotels, which may be ideal if you like a busy town atmosphere. Since this is the hub of the island bus service, it's easy to get public transport to the various walks from here.

The main bus service runs down the eastern side of the island from Rhodes to Líndos, so many resorts on the east coast are well placed for bus connections. Moving down the eastern side of the island, **Kalithéa** is a relatively small resort, but the next one, Faliráki, is much bigger. In spite of bad press over recent years, **Faliráki** is still a great resort with perhaps the best beach on the island. For a peaceful existence, choose a hotel on the outskirts. There are some good hotels located on the coastal strip just north of Faliráki — just keep out of the centre at night. In any case, it's a very quiet resort in the walking season and only becomes rowdy in the height of summer when the party animals arrive in numbers. Now with a permanent police presence in the resort, the troublesome element has been mostly eliminated.

Still on the east coast, and south of Faliráki, lie **Afándou** and **Kolímbia**. These two resorts have been growing steadily in recent years, but are not large like Faliráki. Many, but not all buses running between Rhodes and Líndos call in at Kolímbia Beach, but it's reasonably well served in season. Afándou is more of a problem: buses run along the main road behind the resort, but at present don't turn off along the beach road, so it's at least a 10-15 minute walk to the beach.

The second cluster of resorts is well down the eastern side of the island — Líndos, Péfkos and Lárdos. **Líndos**, lying in a sweeping bay overlooked by an ancient acropolis, is a spectacular resort and a 'must' place to visit. It's one of the two excursions we have chosen. **Péfkos** and **Lárdos** lie a little further south. Although well connected by bus to Rhodes Town, these two resorts are a little remote from our walks, the only two neaby being Walks 8 and 11.

What to take

There is no special dress code for dining, except that shorts are not always appreciated in restaurants and some tavernas during the evening. It's useful for men to pack at least one tie, on a just-in-case basis, especially if a casino visit is on the cards.

It's more important to concentrate on packing suitable walking gear. Walking boots are the footwear we most strongly recommend, but not all the walks demand them. Some of the track walks are fairly easy underfoot, and for these we prefer **walking shoes** or specialist walking trainers, especially if the weather is hot. Each person should carry a **small rucksack** and it's advisable to pack it with a **sunhat**, **suncream**, **first-aid kit** and some extra **warm clothing**. A **long-sleeved shirt** and **long trousers** should be worn or carried for sun protection and for walking through spiny vegetation. You should always carry a **mobile phone**; the **emergency number** on Rhodes (as throughout the EU) is 112.

Depending on the season, you may also need light-weight **rainwear** and a light-weight folding **umbrella**. Some of our walks end up at a beach, so **swimwear** could be usefully included. A reliable litre-size **water bottle** is well worth packing, although

Beach bar, Ixiá

small, easily carried bottles of water can be bought all over the island. *It is imperative that each walker carries at least a half-litre of water — a full litre or more when the weather is hot.*

Planning your walks

Look over the walks you plan to take in advance, to check out **transport**. Most of the walks can be reached by public transport, but the remainder will require a hire car or taxi.

We have **graded** the walks with the weekend walker in mind, based on an ambient temperature *below the mid 20s C.* When temperatures rise above this level, walkers expend more energy simply keeping cool, and uphill walking especially is much more tiring. The **walking times** given at certain points always refer to the total walking time from the start and are based on an average rate of 4km per hour and allowing an extra 15min for every 100m/330ft of ascent. These time checks are not intended to predetermine your own pace but are meant to be useful reference points. A walk might easily take you *twice as long* if you dawdle over the scenery, nature-watch or stop for the thousand little reasons which bring walkers to a halt.

Our walking **maps** are based in part on the Road Editions map mentioned on page 29 and in part on very old military maps showing contours and some physical features. All the base maps have been heavily annotated and updated by our notes in the field. We have enlarged our maps to a scale of 1:40,000 to include a bit more detail, but the only paths shown on our maps are those we *know* to be viable.

Walking safely depends in great part on *knowing what to* *expect and being properly equipped.* For this reason we urge you to read through the *whole* walk description at your leisure *before* setting out, so that you have a mental picture of each stage of the route and the landmarks. One or two of these walks are waymarked, but **waymarks** may be found along parts of the others. *Only follow waymarks if they are confirmed by the route description.*

Thunderstorms in late autumn, after a long summer drought, can cause **flash flooding**, potentially a serious danger to walkers. Keep an eye on the forecast at this time of the year and do not take risks with the weather.

ON ARRIVAL
Tourist information

The main **tourist office** (EOT) is in Rhodes Town, at the corner of Makariou and Papagou [1 on the plan inside the front cover]. Ask for the following; they are all free: bus timetables; opening hours/admission prices (for archaeological sites and other attractions); timetables for boat trips to various islands; map of the island (including a map of the Old Town and a list of useful telephone numbers).

The most useful **map of the island** is the 1:100,000 Road Editions map (No 202) which can be bought on the island or at home before you go.

Transport

There is a very good **bus service** on Rhodes, both within the city and out to surrounding towns and villages. There are frequent

services out of Rhodes Town to popular destinations like
Faliráki and Líndos, but this changes according to demand.
Regularly updated timetables are available from the tourist
office (see above). Unfortunately, there is still no web site for
bus timetables.

Taxis are easily found in Rhodes Town and most other
tourist centres. When three or four people are sharing, they can
be reasonably cheap and a more convenient option than the
bus. Most taxi drivers on Rhodes speak English, so you should
be able to establish the fare before setting out — or make sure
the journey is being metered.

Shopping for self-catering

Most self-catering accommodation on Rhodes is limited to
facilities for throwing breakfast together. There are usually two
hot plates combined with a fridge unit, and cooking utensils are
minimal. There was a time — very recently — when we
calculated that it was better value to eat out than buy food to
cook yourself. It may not hold
true now, but it's not so much
more expensive to dine out in
a taverna.

Few people want to waste
warm evenings cooking when
they could be out enjoying the
atmosphere. There are one or

Street-trader with bread rings
(*kouloúria*)

30

two meals which can be assembled quickly without toiling in the heat. Salads are easy enough to put together, and most supermarkets have a **vegetable** section of some kind. Larger supermarkets offer a better choice of fresh vegetables — as do the local outdoor markets. Lettuce, tomatoes, onions, cucumbers and peppers are basics which most supermarkets stock. Remember these are often **local produce** and are *not treated or sprayed* in any way to make them look or stay fresh, so they may look a little sad towards the end of the day.

This selection of fresh vegetables is typical of a good Rhodes Town supermarket

Freshly barbecued chicken is also available daily and always a good start for a basic meal. Some of the dips, like *tzatzíki* and *taramasaláta,* can be bought ready-made but, to make your own *tzatzíki,* head for the **delicatessen** counter and buy the strained yoghurt *(filtráro yiaoúrti)* found in a large white plastic drum. Ask for it by weight: we find a half kilo *(misó kiló)* more than enough for two, and it's packed in a plastic container for you. This is the really thick strained yoghurt used by the tavernas to make their own *tzatzíki,* and it is also ideal for yoghurt and

31

honey. (When making any of our recipes back home, Total yoghurt, made in Greece, is the one to use.)

The delicatessen counter is where you can buy your **cheese**, too, and there is a much larger selection than just *féta*. Avoid *féta* which has been left on display and allowed to dry out. It loses texture and becomes strongly flavoured. Always buy your *féta* from the drum where it has been kept moist under brine. There are a number of hard cheeses to choose from, including *gravéria*, well worth trying if you like gruyère, and *kaséri*. Soft cheeses are *féta* (also available from Total in the UK), *kopanistí* and *myzíthra*. Greeks love their *myzíthra*. This is a low-fat cheese rather like a smooth cottage cheese. If you can buy it unsalted (often available in spring), it's great with honey for breakfast, but for the rest of the year it's usually salted.

Meat and **fish** can be bought from the big supermarkets. Except for octopus, squid, tuna and sword-fish steaks, most species of fish on

---

Supermarket shopping list
washing-up liquid
washing powder for hand washing (look for the hand wash logo on the box and the word *xépi*, the Greek word for 'hand')
olive oil soap (excellent for removing stubborn stains when hand washing)
soap
paper towels and/or napkins
aluminium foil
tissues/toilet paper
scouring pads
salt & pepper
herbs & spices
mineral water
milk
coffee/tea/drinking chocolate
butter
sugar
bread
juice
wine/beer/oúzo
sunflower oil (cooking)
olive oil (salads) & vinegar
eggs
tomato purée
rice/pasta
mayonnaise/mustard

sale may be unfamiliar. In spring and autumn, small fish like whitebait are available, which can be dipped in flour, fried and eaten whole (recipe page 120). Ready-cleaned fish from the freezer offers an easier option for self-catering. Small, ready-made-up *souvláki* (**meat on a spit**) can usually be bought from the meat counter or butchers — handy if you are staying in a complex with a communal barbecue. Similarly, the **sausage** on Rhodes is packed with meat and another great favourite for the barbecue. All the usual selection of chops and chicken pieces is on offer.

G-F, D-F shopping

People on **dairy-free** diets may have few problems finding staples for their needs in large supermarkets, where soya products may be

Vegetarian, vegan, dairy- and gluten-free recipes

The two books listed below contain straightforward recipes for those with special dietary needs. Both are worth considering if you plan to self-cater in Greece, and both are lightweight paperbacks easily packed in your luggage. They are available from www.amazon.co.uk **Greek Vegetarian Cooking** by Alkmini Chaitow is a book with plenty of excellent recipes and menu suggestions. It also indicates which recipes are dairy- and/or gluten-free.

A Vegan Taste of Greece by Linda Majzlik offers plenty of recipes to sample, and a concise, comprehensive listing and description of ingredients. Equally useful for vegetarians and for those on dairy- or gluten-free diets.

Hint: Those with food allergies will find the **Annapolis Inn** on 28th October Street [36 on the plan inside the front cover] sympathetic to their dietary requirements, especially for evening meals booked in advance (ask to speak to Susie).

available. But apart from staples like rice and chick peas, **gluten-free** food is much harder to find. Gluten intolerance is little recognised and rarely diagnosed on Rhodes, although there is a growing awareness. However, two **health food shops** in Rhodes Town should cater for all requirements admirably — as well as being of interest to **vegetarians** and **vegans**. *To Panéri* [Pavlou Mela 17, (22410 35877; 29 on the town plan inside the front cover] has an excellent g-f selection — from flours through to ready-made corn bread, pasta, rice cakes, biscuits, and cereals (including organic muesli). English is spoken there too, which is a big help. A second source is *Bioeyeia Biooikoloyia* [28th October Street 18, (22410 31416; 30 on the plan]. The name roughly translates to 'healthy organic food'. This shop, near the Annapolis Inn, also stocks a range of vegan, dairy-free and gluten-free products and, again, some English is spoken.

Rhodes market

The market used to be held in the Moorish building at Mandráki Harbour, and the old fish market can still be seen in the middle, but the slabs remain empty these days. The main outdoor market [34 on the town plan] is now much larger and lies on the eastern side of town, on Annas Marias Street, next to the main cemetery. Held every Wednesday and Friday, it's a large and colourful affair, with fresh vegetables of every description, fruit, cheese, olives, clothing and just about everything else. Make sure you go in the morning (the earlier the better), as stalls close down rapidly in the afternoon. Fish, poultry and eggs, etc are sold in the shops just across the road.

Even if you are not shopping, it's a fascinating snapshot of Greek culture and the way of life ... and it's hard to believe you will come away without something!

There is a Thursday market [35 on the plan], too, held off Venetokieon Street, due south of the Old Town walls outside the Diágoras football stadium.

A visit to the main market could be incorporated into the walk round the outside of the town walls (Walk 2). We followed narrow Mitropoleos Street from behind Diágoras Stadium straight there. Returning along the coast road (not very riveting initially, but better as you near the Old

Commercial Harbour

Town walls), we passed some interesting fish tavernas and *oúzeries*. This route also provides a good opportunity to see the Commercial Harbour, where there is often some interesting shipping on view. You can then enter the Old Town through the Marine Gate for more browsing.

This medieval fortress town is the best preserved of its kind in Europe and teems with history and stories around every corner. We never tire of wandering these streets. For more in-depth information it's advisable to consult a general guide book, like our own *Visitor's Guide to Rhodes* (2005 edition).

rhodes old town

Start the walk at the north end of **Mandráki Harbour**, using the plan inside the front cover. Developed during the Italian era, Mandráki, with its Italianate buildings and medieval windmills, is the most attractive of the town's three harbours. From the **Church of the Evangelist** [7] on the promenade, almost level with harbour entrance, head in the direction of the old walled town. The harbour entrance is reputed to have been the site of the Colossus of Rhodes, but the more gentle stag and doe emblems of the island now stand watch. Tucked into a corner by the post office [5] is the easily missed **Café People & People** [31; see page 46]. The Turkish-style *Nea Agorá* [6; '**New Market**'] — now a misnomer as the markets have been moved — is mainly given over to tavernas and cafés.

Distance: 5km/3mi; allow half a day

Grade: easy level walking, with limited uphill sections

Transport: 🚌 into Rhodes Town; many buses from outlying areas head for the town in the morning and return in the afternoon. Or taxi to Alexandrias Square, next to the 'New Market'. 🚗 It is almost impossible to park near the centre, except early Sunday morning. There are blue pay-and-display zones, but street parking just outside the centre provides the best opportunity, especially during school holidays. Be prepared to have to walk a little way into the centre.

Refreshments: huge choice; we've selected a few favourites (see pages 46-49)

Opening times/entry fees:
Archaeological Museum & Pythári (next door), one ticket for both €3; 08.30-14.30; cl Monday
Palace of the Knights €6; daily 08.30-19.00 (Mondays 12.30-19.00)
Museum of Decorative Arts €2; 08.30-14.30; cl Monday
Byzantine Museum (Panagía Kástrou) €2; 08.30-14.30; cl Monday
Note: an economical €10 ticket covers entrance to all the above museums.

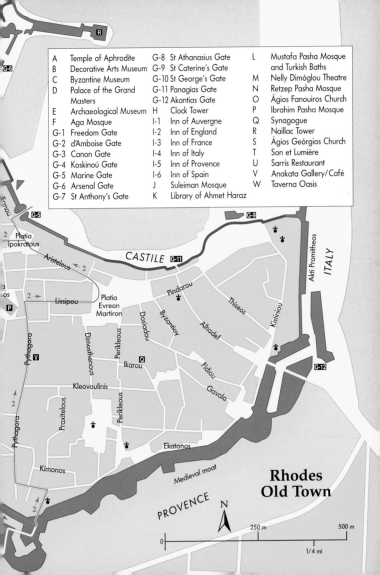

A	Temple of Aphrodite	G-8	St Athanasius Gate	L	Mustafa Pasha Mosque and Turkish Baths
B	Decorative Arts Museum	G-9	St Caterine's Gate	M	Nelly Dimóglou Theatre
C	Byzantine Museum	G-10	St George's Gate	N	Retzep Pasha Mosque
D	Palace of the Grand Masters	G-11	Panagías Gate	O	Ágios Fanouiros Church
E	Archaeological Museum	G-12	Akantias Gate	P	Ibrahim Pasha Mosque
F	Aga Mosque	H	Clock Tower	Q	Synagogue
G-1	Freedom Gate	I-1	Inn of Auvergne	R	Naillac Tower
G-2	d'Amboise Gate	I-2	Inn of England	S	Ágios Geórgios Church
G-3	Canon Gate	I-3	Inn of France	T	Son et Lumière
G-4	Koskinoú Gate	I-4	Inn of Italy	U	Sarris Restaurant
G-5	Marine Gate	I-5	Inn of Provence	V	Anakata Gallery/Café
G-6	Arsenal Gate	I-6	Inn of Spain	W	Taverna Oasis
G-7	St Anthony's Gate	J	Suleiman Mosque		
		K	Library of Ahmet Haraz		

Rhodes Old Town

PROVENCE

N

0   250 m   500 m

1/4 mi

The slabs of the old fish market in the centre are now museum pieces (but the toilets beneath are clean and free). An excellent kiosk for fresh *pitas* (pies) is located in the exit onto Alexandrias Square. A walk out past the **windmills** [21] to **Ág Nikólaos lighthouse** [8] allows for a closer view of the yachts and a good overview of the Italian architecture along the waterfront.

Cross **Platia Alexandrias** and continue ahead past sponge-sellers and artists to enter the Old Town, along with the traffic, via Freedom Gate [9; G-1 on the plan on pages 38-39]. The traffic soon hurtles away to the left, as pedestrians enter the **Collachium** (Knights' Quarters). On the left are the remains of a 3rd-century BC **Temple of Aphrodite** [A] then, a little further along, the **Inn of Auvergne** [I-1; 1507]. The building on the right, cloaked in a tumble of bougainvillaea and with a Byzantine baptismal font serving as a fountain, was the first Hospital of the Knights. It was also used by them and later by the Turks as an arsenal. Today it houses the delightful folk art **Museum of Decorative Arts** [B]. Opposite is the Byzantine Church of St Mary, with a chequered history: it was the first Cathedral of the Knights, then converted to a mosque, reconverted to a Christian church, and is now the **Byzantine Museum** [C].

Sponges make a good buy to take home.

Cobbled Odos Ipoton (Street of the Knights), along which the 'inns' of the various 'tongues' were sited, rises to the right, to the **Palace of the Grand Masters** [D]. From here Walk 2 visits the city walls; see page 43. The impressive building just beyond Odos Ipoton, also on the right, was the new Hospital of the Knights. It now serves as the **Archaeological Museum** [E] and is worth more than a glance. Inside is the Marine Venus, a statue of Aphrodite which inspired Lawrence Durrell's book *Reflections on a Marine Venus.*

Ahead now is the more colourful bustle of Sokratous Street with its old Turkish bazaar atmosphere. A left leads towards the Commercial Harbour and the Jewish Quarter, both of which can be explored on Walk 2. Heading right, you pass projecting

Entrance to the Palace of the Grand Masters. The Knights Hospitallers of St John was founded as a nursing order in the 11th century by Italian merchants, to care for Christian pilgrims en route to Jerusalem. They survived on Rhodes for 500 years before the Turks drove them away. The Knights were divided into seven 'tongues' *(langues):* France, Provence, Auvergne, Spain, Italy, Germany and England, under a Grand Master whom they elected. Later seven became eight when Spain was subdivided into Aragon and Castile. Each tongue operated from its own headquarters or 'inn'.

wooden balconies, intriguing peaceful alleyways and, on the right, a traditional Turkish tea house. Hidden by an arch of the **Aga Mosque** [F], which juts into the street, the Suleiman Mosque, complete with recently restored minaret, dominates the view ahead. Beyond the mosque there are choices to be made. To the right leads to the Palace of the Grand Masters (another chance to get to the start of Walk 2) and the top end of Odos Ipoton, while ahead is *To Roli* [the **Clock Tower**; H] and **d'Amboise Gate** [G-2].

Turn left into Ipodamou, where **Suleiman Mosque** [J] is on the right, to pass the Turkish Library of **Ahmet Havuz** [K] on the right. Divert briefly left, by the Symposium Garden Restaurant, to the **Mustafa Pasha Mosque** and **Turkish Baths** [L] of the same name in Platia Arionas. Behind the baths is the **Nelly Dimóglou Theatre** [M], the best place to see performances of Greek dancing. Continue along Ipodamou and, before reaching the town walls and passing the St Nicholas Hotel on the left, turn left and wend your way into Omirou.

Pass the end of Fanouriou (on the left), but turn left soon afterwards through an archway, into Platia Dorieos with its domed fountain and the **Retzep Pasha Mosque** [N]. The old Byzantine church of **Ágios Fanoúrios** [O] is masked by **Taverna Oasis** [W; see page 46], where the leafy, shaded tables and peaceful ambience makes for an ideal lunch stop. To complete the walk, go left beyond Taverna Oasis into Fanouriou and turn right. Fanouriou is one of the oldest streets and rises back into Sokratous by the **Aga Mosque** [F].

Buy your ticket at the **Palace of the Grand Masters** [D], then head for the steps leading to the gate onto the walls. With the crowds heading off towards distant horizons, you can enjoy a far more peaceful stroll. Climb the steps and go through small **Canon Gate** [G-3], then along the walled path, to reach the outer walls. The walls were divided between the 'tongues', who were responsible for the defence of their particular section (called 'curtains'). This walk passes along the curtains of Auvergne, Aragon and England — in that order.

The Palace of the Grand Masters sits on the highest part of the Collachium (Knights Quarters) and was built on the probable site of the Sanctuary of Helios, the sun god long associated with Rhodes. The rest of the town, more colourful and less

old town walls

WALK

Palace of the Grand Masters, To Roli and Suleiman Mosque, seen from the old walls

austere than the Collachium, was called the Bourg and occupied by the merchants. It's interesting to note the scattering of minarets from the Turkish era, many of which have been and are still undergoing restoration, and to overlook the narrow maze of streets. You also have a fine view over the walls themselves — their actual shape and construction. The moat surrounding the walls was left dry deliberately. The complex structure of the entrance gates, designed to make access almost impossible for invaders, is also best observed from above.

The wall walk ends at **Koskinoú Gate** [G-4]. Descend the steps and stay ahead to a T-junction. Go left (but you may choose to go right) and head right along Pythagora, back into the hub of the Old Town. Bougainvillaea-shaded **Anakata Gallery** [V; see page 48], opposite an excavated section of Byzantine fortification walls, offers a welcome retreat along Pythagora.

See map on pages 38-39
Distance: 4km/2.5mi; allow about 2h; the section atop the walls is about 1.7km/ 1mi; the rest of the walk is inside the walls.

Grade: easy. Although the wall is unfenced on the inside, it's very wide, with no danger of vertigo — but children should be held in check. Steps at the start and end of the wall walk.

Opening times/entry fees:
Palace of the Grand Masters
Open Tue & Sat at 14.45. €6 from the ticket kiosk at the main entrance

Further along on the left is the **Ibrahim Pasha Mosque** [P] in pleasant Platanos Square. A right from here along Lisipou leads to **Platia Evreon Martiron**, the square of the Jewish Martyrs, with its fountain of bronze sea horses. The square was renamed in memory of the remaining Jewish population who were deported to German concentration camps from that spot in 1943. Continue along Aristotelous, through Platia Ipokratous into Ermou and the **Gate of Thálasini** [**Marine Gate**; G-5]. Venture out through the gates here to see the **Commercial Harbour,** where cruise liners and the ocean-going yachts of the rich and famous dock. Further along to the right is the quieter **Akándia Port**. Return through the medieval gateway and follow Sokratous a short distance to Platia Evdimou and **Sarris Restaurant** [U; see page 48], after which a right turn leads back to **Freedom Gate** and exit close to **Platia Alexandrias**.

People & People

Tucked into a corner next to the post office at a busy T-junction, this café is *not* a tourist venue, but very popular with the locals. Drinks are reasonably priced but the tempting snacks more pricey. Good place to sit and watch the world go by.

People & People

Pane di Capo

Another café well frequented by the locals. To find it, walk uphill from Alexandrias Square, then turn right along the next street after the toilets on the left. A tented area adjacent to the café, on the right, makes it easy to spot.

PEOPLE & PEOPLE CAFÉ
25th Martirou €€

In summer, a *frappé* goes down well, and in the food stakes there is a choice of *pitas* (small savoury pies), sandwiches and *bougátza* (chocolate muffins), chocolate mousse or ice creams

Taverna Oasis

This really is an oasis within the teaming maze of narrow streets in Old Rhodes Town. By the time you reach here you'll

PANE DI CAPO CAFÉ
corner of Tarpon & Karpathos €€

large selection of drinks, sandwiches, *pitas* (small savoury pies) and cakes

be more than ready to relax in the somnolent surroundings of Platia Dorieos. The wide-ranging, moderately priced menu comes with an English translation of Greek specialities and lists ingredients.

restaurants

eat

The owner honestly told us that the *kalámari* was frozen, but it was the tenderest frozen *kalámari* we've ever had (see page 12 for more about *kalámari*). Of course red wine is also available, but we find white at lunch time less sleep-inducing (read more about wine on page 20). While chips are not part of our normal daily fare, we do indulge when in Greece, as they go so well with fish dishes.

Some starters: cheese dip, stuffed peppers and black olive paste at the Varkarola Taverna (see page 51)

Around the corner from Oasis, on Odos Fanouriou, is the pleasant **Nísiros Taverna** in a walled garden setting. We haven't eaten there, but there is an abundance of similar tavernas within the Old Town walls, all with similar menus. Some are frankly rip-off joints (as we found to our cost). Watch out for comments like 'If you don't like the food you will only pay for the wine': you will find that the price of the wine alone — even house wine in a jug — is astronomical. *Always check prices before you order.* Most establishments are moderate in price, especially the more off the beaten tourist route you go.

> **TAVERNA OASIS**
> **Platia Dorieos** (2241 034253
> daily, 'morning, noon and night', at
> least in the season €€
>
> try the excellent **Greek salad** of
> lettuce, tomatoes, peppers, cucumber, olives and *féta* cheese, followed by fried *kalámari* and chips
> (*patátes tiganetés*) — all washed
> down with the excellent white house
> wine. Their *kalámari* is shown on
> page 83.

Anakata Gallery

This small, intimate, bougainvillaea-shaded courtyard can be easily missed even though it fronts Pythagora. It was the tumble of bougainvillaea which stopped us in our tracks and lured us in for rest and refreshment. Although a little more pricey than some (€€), it's worth it for the ambience.

Besides the usual beverages there is a fruit punch (with or without alcohol), cakes, fruit salad and ice cream. For something more substantial than the usual sandwiches and pies, there are cold plates of meat, cheese and salad, etc.

Sarris Restaurant

Close to the hub of movement through the Old Town, but tucked to one side of quieter Platia Evdimou, Sarris has an extensive Greek and international menu. Snacks and drinks are also available outside main meal times, and their *frappé* is one of the best we've enjoyed on Rhodes.

Here's a chance to really go to town and try something different from the usual taverna fare. How about *saligária yiáxni* (snails in tomato sauce) — or you can just have them with garlic butter if you prefer. Dishes range in price

> **SARRIS RESTAURANT**
> **corner of Socratous & Evdimou, 18**
> **Old Rhodes Town** (2241 073707
> **cl mid-Dec till mid-Feb** €€-€€€
>
> some menu highlights:
>
> **snails and mussels** served in a variety of ways
>
> **cockles, Sími shrimps**, baby shrimps in garlic sauce, marinated **octopus** — and even a delectable speciality **sea urchin** salad (*axionó saláta*; sea urchins are a special treat in Greece)
>
> ample **steak and meat** dishes
>
> plenty of **Greek specialities**, including *soutzoukákia* (spicy meat rolls)

restaurants

eat

downwards from the expensive to very reasonable, so your wallet doesn't need to be hurt too much.

Léski Restaurant

Located in an old mansion and its garden, this is predominantly a place where the Greeks go once they've finished work. A lunchtime gem for Grecophiles, but don't necessarily expect to find much English spoken. There is no menu, so you'll have to discover for yourself what's on offer. An invitation to visit the kitchen to choose from the limited number of excellent dishes cooked daily is usual for those not fluent in Greek. Surprisingly, it's a world away from the bustle one would expect so close to Rhodes Town. The Palace of the Grand Masters can be seen through the trees. Umbrellas shade diners in the courtyard, while trees act as natural umbrellas in the garden area. If the weather is inclement, there is seating inside.

Outdoor dining at Léski

LESKI RESTAURANT
corner of Naviarinou & Riga Feriou,
west of St George's Tower
lunch and dinner €€

besides **salads**, there may be different types of **mezédes** on offer as well.

typical menu entries for **main courses** include:

beef or pork & mushrooms in lemon sauce; *keftédes* in white sauce; *briám* and cabbage *dolmádes* all served with chips or rice and a delicious Greek salad

recommended **house wine**

There are many pleasant tavernas you could choose from just outside Rhodes Town, but the three mentioned here are places we particularly like; they are all easy places to stop after a day out, and especially enjoyable for Grecophiles.

Varkarola Taverna (part of the Rodian Beach Amathus Hotel complex)

Tucked into the hillside at Ixiá, the Rodian Beach (www.rodian-beach.gr) is a recent acquisition of the Cyprus-based Amathus Hotel group of five-star hotels offering a high level of comfort and amenities. Within easy distance of Rhodes Town and the airport, it makes a good venue for weddings, conferences, family get-togethers and holidays. The icing on the cake is the excellent level of catering generally (with special attention to dietary needs), and an evening meal at the hotel's Varkarola Taverna is a special treat.

The Varkarola is a relaxing place to be for that special evening meal or light lunch and is open to the general public. There is no need to book for lunch, but evening bookings are essential.

We have spent time here on two occasions and enjoyed both the Friday night Lobster Evening and Tuesday's Greek Evening in the hotel, with food and dancing. The Varkarola is accessible from the beach via a tunnel under the road, for those wishing to call in for lunch. The beach stretches all the way from Rhodes Town to Triánda, so covers a wide-ranging catchment area. Taxis are cheap and easily available for those visiting in the evening.

A selection from the evening menu is shown opposite; there is a lighter lunch-time selection. A good choice of wines is on offer but our favourite, especially with fish, is the white Geravassaliou from Thessaloníki.

restaurants

eat

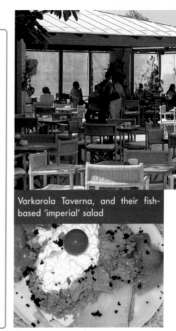

VARKAROLA TAVERNA
Rodian Beach Amathus Hotel
(22410 89900 (hotel reception)
lunch 12.00-15.00 and dinner
20.00-23.30; all meals à la carte
€€-€€€, except the Friday Lobster
Evening

just a few dishes from the evening
menu:

appetizers – carpaccio of
salmon and sea bass; smoked fillet
of duck

salads – 'imperial' salad: smoked
salmon and halibut, with caviar,
cottage cheese and rocket

main courses – breast of
pheasant, flambéd with Grand
Marnier, and lemon grass sauce;
fillet of monkfish with curry sauce
and coconut milk; various pork and
lamb dishes

good choice of **desserts**,
including their brilliant chocolate
soufflé with sauce anglaise (see
recipé on page 55)

Varkarola Taverna, and their fish-
based 'imperial' salad

There was a surprise in store for us when we asked for a recipe at the Varkarola. It was a delicious, mouth-watering hot chocolate soufflé. The restaurant was delighted with our interest, and we were invited to meet the chef the following day for a demonstration. Unfortunately, that did not include another taste of the soufflés, since they need to be chilled for several hours before cooking. We have the recipe for you on page 55. It's so easy to prepare that we now make it on a regular basis when entertaining friends.

Yiannis Taverna

A Greek taverna in the atmospheric, narrow streets of Koskinoú, with eating areas both inside and out. Choose from an extensive menu after first looking round the kitchen to see what they're cooking. Located on the main village street, just south of the church.

YIANNIS TAVERNA
main street, Koskinoú €€

Some different dishes include:
spetzofáï (sausage & peppers in spicy sauce)
seftaliá (homemade sausage)
kondosoúvli (spiced pork on the soúvla or spit)
There is also pork in wine, goat, *kokkinistó*, squid and octopus, etc.
good **house wine** in a jug

Before going to Yiannis to eat, it's worth having a look at the 'Traditional House of Koskinoú' — just a few doors from Yiannis, on the same side of the road (open 10.00-13.00 and 18.00-20.00; cl weekends; entrance is free).

restaurants
eat

Profítis Ámos

Don't be put off by the fact that it's in Faliráki; this really is an unexpected haven, far away from the bustle of Faliráki centre. This taverna, a warm-weather-only venue, is on the site of an old monastery complex dedicated to the Prophet Amos. You can sit outside on a terrace tucked into the hillside with an elevated view over the surrounding countryside.

To find it, turn seawards at the staggered junction traffic lights on the southern edge of Faliráki (opposite the road inland to Kalithiés). Fork right immediately, then take the second right (which may have a signpost to Moní Ámos). Stay on this road as it leads towards the hillside and the taverna at the end.

PROFITIS AMOS
Faliráki (2241 087250
summer only €€

good selection of **mezés** and **grills**
good **white house wine**

The cheerful chef at Profítis Ámos insisted that Eileen had her photo taken with the octopus he was soon to barbecue.

53

Briám (Baked vegetables)

A popular dish on taverna menus, *briám* is akin to a baked ratatouille, a vegetable dish of mainly potato, courgette and aubergine — with additions to taste. Our recipe is easy, but to make a traditional *briám,* layer the vegetables (see below).

Place the vegetables and peppers in a baking dish. Mix together all the other ingredients and pour over. Cover and bake at 180° C/ gas mark 4 for 1 hour or more.

Layered version: Slice all the vegetables, even the garlic. Start with all the potato layered on the bottom, then the other vegetables, separately, beginning with half the onion. Sprinkle salt, pepper, some garlic, herbs and a drizzle of olive oil over each layer. Finish with a tomato layer; pour over 150 ml stock; Season again to taste. Cover and bake at 190° C/gas mark 5 for about 1 h 15 min. Add extra water if needed.

Optional: Crumble *féta* cheese over the top 20 min before the dish is ready, but cut down the salt in the main dish, as *féta* is quite salty on its own.

Ingredients (for 4 people)
2 large aubergines, in chunks
2 large courgettes, in chunks
3 medium potatoes, cubed
1 green pepper, sliced
1 red pepper, sliced
1 or 2 sticks celery, in chunks
1 medium onion, chopped
2 garlic cloves, crushed
125 ml olive oil
125 ml stock (or water)
4 large tomatoes, skinned & chopped (or 1 tin chopped)
1 tsp oregano
1 tbsp fresh parsley, chopped
salt & pepper

recipes

eat

Poltós eliás mávri (Black olive paste), *illustrated on page 47*

Although this paste, dating from ancient times, is served with bread as a *mezé* at the start of meals at the Rodian Beach Amathus, this recipe isn't from the hotel. Delicious with bread (instead of butter), at the start of a meal or for breakfast. Very easy to make.

Whizz together in a food processor 200 g pitted black olives, 2 garlic cloves, 1 tbsp oregano (or coriander, thyme or cumin), 2 tbsp fresh lemon juice, and 4 tbsp olive oil — until you have a paste. Will store in the fridge for a few days — or pack in small quantities and freeze.

Chocolate soufflé pudding

Have ready 6 crème caramel or small pudding basins (175 ml size), lightly greased and dusted with the cocoa powder.

Beat together the butter and sugar, then beat in the eggs. Melt the chocolate, gently, either over a pan of hot water or on low in the microwave. Add to the above mixture and continue mixing well together. Slowly mix in the vanilla essence and flour and continue mixing until everything is well blended.

Use a spoon or icing bag to fill each basin 2/3 full. Cover and refrigerate for at least 3 h or overnight (the mixture will freeze for 10 days). Bake at 180° C/gas mark 4 for 8-9 min; serve immediately with cream, yoghurt or ice cream.

Ingredients (for 6 people)
125 g butter
100 g icing sugar
4 eggs
cocoa powder for dusting the
    pudding basins
125 g dark chocolate (70%+
    cocoa solids)
two drops vanilla essence
65 g plain flour

Hoirinó kai manitária me lemóni
(Pork and mushrooms with lemon)

Coat the meat in flour and fry in oil with the salt, pepper and cumin. Add the mushrooms, onion, coriander and basil. Stir in the wine.

Transfer to a casserole and cook, covered, in the oven at 170°C/ gas mark 3 for around 1 h 15 min (checking after about 45 min and adding more liquid — either water or wine — if needed). After 1 h 15 min add the lemon juice and return to the oven for a further 10 min.

Serve with rice, pasta, mashed potatoes or chips.

The dish served at Léski Restaurant, where you can dine under the trees

Ingredients (for 4 people)
700 g lean pork in 2.5cm cubes
200 g mushrooms (sliced)
2 large onions
2 tsp dried basil
2 tsp ground cumin
2 tsp ground coriander
500 ml white wine or chicken
   stock
4 tbsp fresh lemon juice

recipes

eat

Soutzoukákia
(Spicy meat rolls)

This recipe, which we photo-graphed at Sarris Restaurant, makes 12 *soutzoukákia*, three for each person.

Mix all the ingredients thoroughly in a large bowl, then add enough egg to bind the mixture so that it doesn't crumble. Divide the mixture into 12 balls and roll in the palm of the hand to bind well, then form into sausage shapes.

Lightly flour the sausage shapes and shallow fry in oil until they are brown on the outside and more or less cooked through. Drain on kitchen paper. In the meantime, make the tomato sauce.

Put all the ingredients for the sauce in a pan and bring to the boil. Simmer gently for about 30 min. Add more red wine and/or passata if required.

When the sauce is ready, add the cooked sausages to the pan and heat for 10 min.

Serve with pasta, rice, chips or mashed potatoes — and peas or other green vegetable.

Ingredients (for 4 people)
400 g minced beef
35 g stale breadcrumbs
1 small onion, finely chopped
1 garlic clove, crushed
1 tbsp fresh thyme (1 tsp dried)
1 tbsp fresh oregano (1 tsp dried)
1/4 tsp ground cumin
1 small egg, lightly beaten
salt & pepper

Tomato sauce (easy version)
125 ml sieved tomatoes (passata or small tin of chopped tomatoes)
75 ml red wine (or extra sieved tomato)
2 tbsp olive oil
1 small garlic clove, crushed
1/2 tsp dried oregano
salt & pepper

Petaloúdes — The Valley of the Butterflies — is one of the island's top tourist attractions, so it's unlikely you will find yourself alone in the valley. But many of the organised tours only walk a short way downhill, then it's back to the coach — so the crowds thin quickly. And very few tourists visit Moní Kalópetra up the hill.

petaloúdes
WALK

It's unusual for a butterfly to become a top tourist attraction, and even more unusual when the star attraction is not a butterfly at all — but a colourful moth, the Jersey tiger moth, *Euplagia quadripunctaria*. It's easy to pass dozens of them resting on the dark bark of the trees, but only when yours eyes become accustomed will you realise that there are hundreds of them all around you. And only when they are in flight will you appreciate their colours. The tree which attracts this lovely moth to this particular valley is the liquidamber tree, *Liquidamber orientalis*. Its leaf looks very like the plane tree, *Platanos orientalis*, except much smaller.

During the 'butterfly' season, visitors are requested to refrain from making sudden

Distance: 4.3km/2.7mi; allow 1h30min-2h

Grade: easy-moderate, with a height gain of 110m/360ft. The entire route is along a path (cobbled in parts). Good shade. *Note that smoking is not allowed in the valley.*

Equipment: see page 27

Transport: 🚌 from Rhodes Town to Petaloúdes (summer only): departs from [3] on the town plan at 09.30 and 11.30; returns at 10.15, 12.15 and 15.00. Or 🚗 car or taxi to the lower entrance at Petaloúdes (limited parking close to Taverna Petaloúdes, otherwise park above in the large car park and walk down the access road to the start of the walk).

Refreshments: Ample refreshment stops during high season: Taverna Petaloúdes at the start; a café/bar at the upper entrance; drinks and light refreshments at Moní Kalópetra

Opening times/entry fee: open daily from 08.00 until sunset; entry €3 (mid-Apr to mid-Jun), €5 (mid-Jun to end Sep, when the 'butterflies' are active), €3 end Sep to end Oct. Otherwise entry is free.

noises — like clapping — to make them fly. The disturbance caused by noise is one of the reasons the moths are reducing in numbers. Out of season, it's still a beautiful valley and a worthwhile walk. You may not have the butterflies, but there is more chance of solitude.

The walk starts at the bottom of the valley by **Taverna Petaloúdes**, near the museum. Head uphill through the taverna to the entry booth. Keep your entrance ticket to hand, as it will have to be shown each time a pay booth is passed.

Just continue uphill on the path through the valley, now under good shade. The 'butterflies' can be quite active in this lower section at the height of the season.

Rise through a pleasant café area to reach the **road to Psínthos (15min)**. To the right is a toilet block but go left, briefly, along the road, then head right to continue uphill through the valley. Route-finding isn't a problem as the path heads uphill through the main section of the valley with the opportunity for short diversions. In spring, *Cyclamen repandum* is quite abundant and compensates for the lack of 'butterflies'. In fact, this is one of the best places on the island to find it.

When you come to a further pay booth and a flat area with seating and more toilets (**40min**), follow the paved path to the right. Then go left up steps, to reach the road below Moní Kalópetra. Turn left, then go right into the car park at **Moní Kalópetra** (**50min**). The refreshments are mouth-watering, and there are good toilets.

Petaloúdes Taverna; below: *Cyclamen repandum* and a Jersey tiger moth

Return by the same route, downhill this time, back to **Taverna Petaloúdes** (**1h30min**).

For those with a car, there is an opportunity to visit the nearby Ostrich Farm. Children especially will love this — a lunch of (excellent) ostrich burgers! Finish off with a wine tasting session at the winery, where we particularly enjoyed the red wine; it's close to the access road to the Ostrich Farm.

Moní Kalópetra Café

This café, with a beautiful terrace setting and panoramic views which reach beyond Soroni on the coast, is an ideal spot to soak in the ambience and enjoy some light refreshment.

MONI KALOPETRA CAFÉ
Petaloúdes/Psínthos road €€

very special **Greek salad**

loukoumádes (batter balls in honey) and yoghurt, nuts and honey

fresh orange juice, fresh **figs** (in September)

Moní Kalópetra, with a plane-shaded terrace overlooking the coast

Taverna Pigí Fasoúli

Most visitors only get as far as the cluster of tavernas in Psínthos square, but this was a particularly special find for us. Great for those in search of genuine Greek food, with an extensive menu, very reasonable prices and a quieter location. Pigí Fasoúli (rated 5 out of 5 by Trip Advisor in 2013) lies downhill to the left, a short way along the road from Psínthos to Archípoli. Better still, park in Psínthos square and take this delightful six-minute riverside stroll to the taverna (see opposite).

TAVERNA PIGI FASOULI
Psínthos/Archípoli road €€

the speciality is **sikotariá** (fried pieces of liver and kidney) — it is really, really tasty, *but not shown on the menu!*

also tempting here are **loukániko** (lean and tasty village sausage), **pitaroúdia** (recipe page 62), **kolokithákia** (recipe page 105) and a house speciality dessert, **talagoútes** (recipe page 67)

---

restaurants

eat

From the square go roughly east, to the Petaloúdes road junction on the left. To the right is the hollow, stunted trunk of a once-majestic *Platanos* (plane) tree. Go down the steps here to a fountain area, then keep right and cross the river on stepping stones. Go left, downstream, along the very pleasant and shaded, cobbled path beside the river, which is now on your left. The path crosses back over the river before reaching the plane-shaded *platia* and fountain below the taverna, across the river to your right.

Walk back the same way or, from Pigí Fasoúli, follow the road to the right, then keep right when you come to the Archípoli road, back to the square in Psínthos.

Ostrich Farm and Park

After visiting Petaloúdes, this is a quiet place to wander around, away from the tourist bustle, before you have lunch. The farm nestles in the countryside just over 1km along a road leading left off the Kalamónas/Petaloúdes road. This road is just before the winery of Anastasia Triandáfillou (also on the left), around 1.6km/1mi from Petaloúdes.

Besides plenty of ostriches (the farm raises around 200 a year), there is a monkey, animals and birds from Asia, Australia and India, and a few Rodian deer. In Greek, the male deer is *elefós*, the female *elafína,* and the plural *eláfia.* The deer are very shy creatures and at one time were thought to be extinct, but we actually encountered a mother and baby once while out walking.

The café/restaurant, with adjacent children's playground and souvenir shop, sits in an elevated position, with good views over the surround-

OSTRICH FARM AND PARK
signposted off the Kalamónas/Petaloúdes
road (6945 327 142
open daily all year; admission €3
restaurant/café €€

the speciality is **ostrich meat** (fillet steaks,
burgers, schnitzel and omelettes)

also Greek *mezés*, salads (including Greek),
sandwiches, pizzas, crèpes and ice cream

stifádo (veal and shallot stew) and
revíthia (a village stew of meat, chickpeas,
tomatoes and onions cooked in the oven)
are also available in the cooler months

wine, beer, soft drinks

A juicy ostrich burger — not
just for kids

ing countryside. It's a
restful place for a cup of
coffee, oúzo and *mezédes*
or a light lunch.

Ostrich meat is low
in cholesterol, so it's a healthy lunch option. Try the juicy ostrich
burgers or really go for it and have an ostrich schnitzel. If you
aren't keen on burgers because of the bun, ask for a burger, minus
the bun, and have it with a salad. The meaty burger here is very
moist and delicious. The ostrich omelettes are lovely and light;
unbelievably, an ostrich can lay an egg every two days, and one
ostrich egg makes eight omelettes!

Anastasia Triandáfillou Winery

Near the Ostrich Farm and Petaloúdes, this small organic winery
produces a limited number of high-quality wines. The grapes,
locally grown, include the white *Athíri* and red *Mandilári*.

Although production is on a limited scale, the wines are quite
gluggable and reasonably priced. A visit to taste the wine after the
Ostrich Farm makes a fitting end to a full day. Open daily all year
round from 09.00-19.00, they also sell local honey. (22410 82041,
mobile 6972 506996.

Revíthia sto horiátiki foúrno (Chickpea stew)

Dust the meat in seasoned flour and brown in the olive oil, then set aside.

Soften the onion and garlic in the pan. Stir in the tomato paste, dried oregano, chopped tomato and salt & pepper. Bring to the boil, then add the browned meat.

Re-heat and add extra water if needed. Place in a casserole and cook at 170° C/gas mark 3 for about 1 h.

Remove the casserole from the oven and stir in the chickpeas, then return to the oven for a further 20 min.

Hint: This recipe also works well in a wine-based sauce with pork. Omit the tin of tomatoes and replace with 200 ml of white wine. Add 1 tbsp flour mixed with white wine when the chickpeas are added.

Ingredients (for 4 people)

400 g cooked chickpeas (or 2 x 425 g tins, drained)
1 kg cubed pork or beef
2 medium onions, chopped
2 garlic cloves, crushed
2 x 400 g tins chopped tomatoes
2 tbsp tomato paste
250 ml stock (chicken or beef) — or wine
1 tsp dried oregano
3 tbsp fresh parsley, chopped
1 heaped tsp cumin (optional)
4 tbsp olive oil
salt & pepper

recipes

eat

Pitaroúdia (Chickpea cakes)

Either reconstitute dried chickpeas in cold water for 24 hours, then drain, or use the same quantity of tinned chickpeas. Mash or process the chickpeas, almost to a paste, and mix with the onion, tomato, mint and flour. Season with salt & pepper to taste.

Add just enough liquid to bind together. Shape the mixture into thin round cakes about 7 cm in diameter. Dust with flour and fry in hot sunflower oil (see notes on page 10) on both sides until golden brown.

Hints: Not all *pitaroúdia* contain tomato or courgette. Make sure your version is well seasoned, or they may taste bland. For a spicy version add 1 tsp cumin or curry powder. Another tasty alternative is to use 1 large boiled potato (preferably cooked in its skin before peeling and mashing) in place of the flour — a good use for leftover mashed potato.

Pitaroúdia as we serve them at home

Ingredients (for about 12 cakes)

400 g chickpeas or (2 tins drained weight)
1 large onion, grated
1 large ripe tomato, peeled, deseeded & chopped and/or a grated courgette (optional)
1 tbsp fresh mint or dill, parsley etc, chopped
50 g flour
salt & pepper
1 small egg or a drop of water to bind together (add a little at a time)

recipes

eat

Talagoútes (Pancakes with honey and nuts)

These are basically a small thick pancake topped with honey and nuts, more like a drop scone in size and slightly thicker.

Make the batter by mixing the flour, baking powder and salt. Break the eggs into a hollow in the centre of the flour and gradually mix together, with a little milk if needed, to make a thick batter. The mixture shouldn't spread too much when dropped into the pan. Beat well and leave to stand for a while.

Heat some unsalted butter or light cooking oil in a frying pan. Drop 1 tbsp of the mixture into the pan for each pancake. Cook 2 min, then flip over and cook a further 2 min. Be careful not to cook these thick pancakes at too high a temperature, or they will burn.

Place on a plate and pour over runny honey, then sprinkle with toasted sesame seeds or chopped walnuts. Serve topped with a blob of ice cream or cream.

Suggestion: To make fruity pancakes, add 25 g of sugar to the mix, then fold 125 g of blueberries or raspberries into the batter just before cooking.

<u>Ingredients (for 8 servings)</u>
75 g plain flour
1 tsp baking powder
1/4 tsp salt
2 eggs
milk — a little, to make a
    thick batter
unsalted butter or light oil

Trickling streams, rustic bridges, the scent of pine, a taverna, and a lake feeding seven springs — that's Eftá Pigís. This walk from Archángelos nicely complements a visit to Eftá Pigís — and with Café Cappuccino on hand for a cooling iced chocolate before and/or after the walk, it could hardly start from a better place.

eftá pigís ('seven springs')
WALK

Start the walk in **Archángelos** at the **bridge** over the concrete river bed, opposite the road down to Stegná. Head back north over the bridge in the direction of Rhodes Town and, almost immediately, take the first road turning left (inland). In two minutes, at a fork, stay right (the road to the left is your return route). When you reach the **Archángelos bypass** (**10min**), cross it and continue ahead (signposted 'Eftá Pigís 5km').

The road reverts to track shortly. Ignore a minor track forking left (**18min**), but fork left a minute later (signposted '7 Pigís'). Pass **St George's church**, across the stream bed on the left, then stay with the main track as it bears left over the stream bed and starts to rise. Eventually (**45min**) the track levels out, and a few minutes later it starts descending towards Eftá Pigís.

Distance: 12.3km/7.7mi; 3h30min

Grade: easy-moderate; mainly along tracks, with an overall height gain of 115m/380ft

Equipment: see page 27

Transport: 🚌 to Archángelos (Rhodes/Líndos bus, departures from [2] on the plan; very frequent in the main season). Or 🚗 taxi or car to Archángelos (alight/park near the bridge over the river, on entering Archángelos from Rhodes Town). *Motorists:* see the tip about Savas Pottery on page 70.

Refreshments: café/bars and restaurants in Archángelos; seasonal snack bar/taverna at Eftá Pigís

Shorter walk: Archípoli road — Eftá Pigís — Archángelos. 7.6km/4.8mi; 2h30min. Easy-moderate. 🚗 taxi to the Eftá Pigís road, south of the main Archípoli/Kolímbia road (make sure he doesn't take you all the way to Eftá Pigís). Or take a 🚌 to the Kolímbia junction and walk along the road towards Archípoli (50min or so; *not suitable in hot weather*). Follow the path at the right of the Eftá Pigís road; a stream bed is to your right. Beyond an old water mill, you come to Eftá Pigís (15min). Follow the main walk from the 1h30min-point to the end.

Stay on the main track, ignoring all minor tracks. Pass a small **church** on the right (**1h**) then, four minutes later, fork right on a track sign-posted to '7 Pigís'. Concreted only at the start, this steeply descending track is quite dusty in summer. When you meet a surfaced road (**1h 25min**), turn right, downhill, for a short distance, heading towards the round concrete ventilation shaft on the left. (This shaft ventilates a 180m-long tunnel carrying a water channel between a lake (reservoir) and Eftá Pigís. It is possible to paddle through this tunnel with care — some people do — but it is dark and potentially dangerous; we don't recommend it.)

Savas Pottery

If you are travelling to Archán-gelos by car, a pleasant diversion is to follow the old national road which forks off right 1.6km/1mi south of the Kolímbia junction. This short stretch of road (only around 3km/2mi) passes through rural countryside. Around 1km before rejoining the main road at Archángelos, watch out for the white buildings of Savas on the left. This lovely traditional pottery is open every day in season and Tuesday and Friday afternoons at quieter times. If pottery is your 'thing', telephone 6936607152 or 2244 022292/023361 to make sure the pottery will be open and to see if there may be any hands-on pottery-making demonstra-tions in the offing. Past Savas, a left turn at the main road and then a right turn leads to the start of Walks 4 and 5 in Archángelos.

The track uphill to the right leads to the lake shown on page 68 and some waterfalls, but take the path to the left, before the ventilation shaft, and descend to a track. A right turn here would take you past a water mill to the Archípoli/Kolímbia road, but just to the left is **Eftá Pigís Taverna** (**1h30min**).

Rhodes Town

Archípoli

Loutanis

100

Eftá Pigís

Tunnel

Eftá Pigís Taverna

Kolímbia

351

N

1 km

0.5 mi

0

Ág Fotiní Samarítida

100

National Road

Old

Moní Kyrá Napení

Ág Geórgios

200

Moní Panagía Tsambíkas

Savas Pottery

100

Ág Nikólaos & Néstoras

Líndos

Café Cappuccino

Archángelos

5

5

5

78

Stegná

Stegná Kozas Taverna

Return to Archángelos by descending towards the river, walking across the taverna terrace and crossing the **bridge**. After crossing the bridge, follow the path to the left, initially alongside the Seven Springs, to rise into the pine trees. In seven or so minutes fork right uphill and, two minutes later, again fork right. A good 10 minutes from the taverna, stay ahead towards an olive grove, skirting above it to the left. A minute later, the path widens into a terrace. Keep ahead to meet a very rough crossing track at the far end of the olive grove, and follow this uphill to the left.

The track rises into a large area of **olive groves** (1h45min). Stay left, with a fence on the left and, in a minute or so (beyond a stone terrace wall on the right), strike off diagonally right across the olive grove. You meet a minor track a few minutes later. Turn left and immediately pass **animal pens** on the right. About four minutes along this track, turn right into a narrow track, heading for a long low hill. In under three minutes, almost at the end of the hill, you pass a **fountain** on the left dated 1996. Continue round the base of the hill. Pass between two rocks and, 40m/yds further on, fork left uphill.

You reach a terrace in two-three minutes, but continue uphill to the left. Rising onto a track, opposite a **concrete hut** (2h10min), turn right. Keep to this track as it follows the valley into a U-bend to the right. The valley eventually reduces to a gully, and the track continues past red-domed **Moní Kyrá Napshowní** (2h30min). Keep round to the left when a track joins from the right (2h35min). The track begins to descend, and Archángelos comes into view ahead. As you descend, turn right

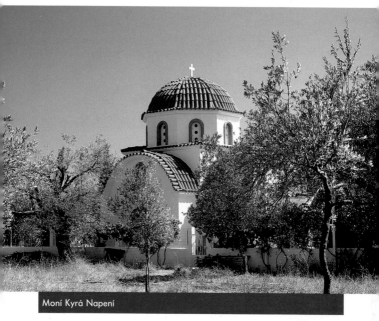

Moní Kyrá Napení

(**2h40min**) into a track with a fence at its left, and keep left when this track forks a few minutes later. Meet a wider track opposite **large metal gates** (**2h55min**) and turn left. Almost immediately, stay left at the fork. Archángelos Castle is seen ahead.

As a track joins from the left (**3h05min**), keep round to the right. The track becomes surfaced before reaching the **bypass road** (**3h15min**). Stay ahead across the bypass, into **Archángelos**. Follow the road alongside the **stadium** wall on the right, then round to the left. When you rejoin your outward route (**3h25min**), head right, back to the **bridge** (**3h30min**).

Café Cappuccino/Zacharoplasteon

An amazing discovery, this café certainly lifts its clients a world away from the traditional and invariably ghastly Greek 'nes'. But the prices aren't over the top. Recline on couches by open windows in summer while enjoying an iced drink. To get there, head a short way southwest along the main street through Archángelos, and the café is on the right-hand corner, beyond the taxi rank. Be sure to specify whether you want your drink hot *(zestos)* or cold *(kreeos)*.

> **CAFÉ CAPPUCCINO**
> **Archángelos (2244 023333**
> **daily all year €€**
>
> huge choice of **chocolate drinks** (classic dark, milk, hazelnut, almond, white, chocolate & coffee, etc), iced teas, *granitas*, ice creams, fondues, cakes and sandwiches …
>
> for **teas** there are various choices like lemon, jasmine, peach, Egyptian flowers … **coffee** lovers will not be disappointed either!

Eftá Pigís Taverna

If lunch in dappled shade accompanied by friendly ducks appeals, then this is the place to be. Open only during the main

> **EFTA PIGIS TAVERNA**
> **Eftá Pigís, only open in season €€**
>
> **bouzákia** (grilled lamb and/or goat) is a speciality offered when the locals are around, otherwise a fairly extensive typical Greek menu

season, the area is a hive of activity, especially at weekends when it's a popular haunt of the Rhodians themselves. The café above is the place for a snack, while the terrace below, just above the river, attracts the diners.

restaurants

eat

A *saganáki* is a small frying pan, usually with two handles, and the food is served in the pan.

Saganáki (Fried cheese) *not illustrated*

Heat butter or light oil in a frying pan until hot. Press the cheese into the flour to coat. Fry in the hot oil for about 1 min each side, until golden brown. Transfer to a warm dish, season with lemon juice and black pepper to taste. Serve immediately.

Tip: Slabs of *haloúmi* cheese (unfloured) can also be grilled. Serve with wedges of lemon.

Féta saganáki sto foúrno (Baked *féta*)

Place the cheese and pepper slices in an ovenproof dish, and put the tomato slices on top. Add a drizzle of olive oil, sprinkle of oregano and black pepper. Wrap the whole thing in a foil parcel – or use a covered clay pot for the baking. Bake at 180° C/gas mark 4 for 15-20 min.

Ingredients (for 4 people)
250 g hard cheese such as *haloúmi*, cut in 10-15 mm-thick slices
lemon juice (to taste)
black pepper, ground
seasoned flour

Ingredients (for 4 people)
400 g *féta* cheese, either sliced or crumbled
1 red or green pepper, finely sliced
2 large tomatoes, thinly sliced
olive oil
oregano
black pepper, ground

recipes

eat

This easy route to Stegná Bay offers especially good views over the bay on the descent, while on the short climb back up, you can visit the church of St George and then look up to Archángelos itself — with its castle crown and the wonderful 'wedding cake' church of the Archangel Michael, which gives the town its name.

archángelos – stegná bay circuit

WALK

Start the walk in **Archángelos** at the **bridge** over the concrete river bed, next to the road down to Stegná. Head down the Stegná road. When the road forks left (**3min**), stay ahead. Then (**7min**) keep round left with the road and, soon afterwards, head into open countryside where the road reverts to track. At a fork (**12min**), go left along a gently rising track (5min further along the main track at this point would take you to the 2h15min-point in the walk — ideal for a very short circular walk taking in the castle).

Now stay ahead on this new track and ignore any forks to the left. As the track rises to a **crest** (**25min**), fork right downhill between rocks and cairns onto a waymarked path. Panoramic views over Stegná Bay open up as the rocky path descends alongside a gulley on the left. This is

Distance: 10km/6.3mi; about 3h

Grade: moderate, with an overall ascent of 200m/650ft. Mainly track, apart from the steep, stony descent to Stegná and the climb back up, which demand agility. *Almost no shade*

Equipment: see page 27

Transport: 🚌 or 🚗 as Walk 4, page 69

Refreshments: Café Cappuccino in Archángelos (see page 74), as well as other cafés and tavernas; selection of cafés and tavernas at Stegná Bay, but don't rely on any being open in Stegná outside the holiday season. Greek friends recommend two tavernas in Archángelos: Savas (☎ 2244 023125) and Afentiká (☎ 2244 023640); we've not had the opportunity to sample them ourselves.

Alternatives: (1) just walk one way, to Stegná (4km/2.5mi; 1h05min; moderate); (2) walk to Stegná and retrace your steps (8km/5mi; 2h30min; moderate); (3) return by bus from Stegná, using a summer-only 🚌 service (check locally); (4) return by taxi; (5) walk back along the road: Stegná Bay stretches for 1km from the harbour before reaching the road to Archángelos, from where it's 3km/1.9mi; 1h uphill back to the start.

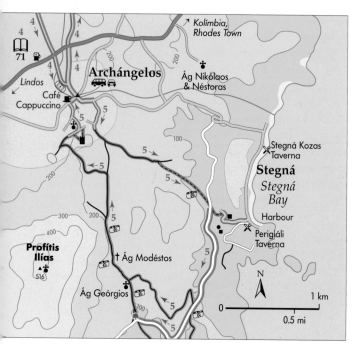

an enjoyable route, but some agility is required. As the waymarks end, cross a stabilised track (or new road) and continue in the same direction through an olive grove. Then head to the back of the large **blue and white apartment block**. Pass behind these apartments (**55min**) and make your way downhill to the **fishing harbour** at **Stegná Bay** (**1h05min**). Our two featured tavernas are To Perigiáli, immediately to the right, and Stegná Kozas, which sits overlooking the shore 1km along the coast road at the far end of the resort, close to where the road enters Stegná from Archángelos.

To continue the walk from To Perigiáli, return to the 55min-point (**1h20min**) and head for a large boulder at the back of a white house beyond the blue and white apartment block. Pass the **boulder** and continue behind the white house. Turn left along the stabilised track (or new road) and follow this up to a crest. Then descend to a fork with a tree in the middle. Take the right-hand, uphill track. (If the road has been surfaced, and you'd like to avoid tarmac wherever

Stegná Bay (top) and descending the path alongside the gulley

possible, see the map for other tracks, highlighted in mauve, which would either shorten or lengthen the walk slightly.) Reach a **high point** (**1h50min**), from where there are excellent views of the coastline and Feraklós Castle atop a rocky outcrop. Beneath the rocky hill ahead is a small white church, your next landfall. Keep along the main track, ignoring tracks left and right, to reach the modern church of **St George (1h55min)**, in a strategic position overlooking the coast. Frescoes adorn the inside walls.

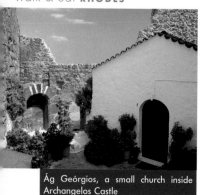

Ág Geórgios, a small church inside Archangelos Castle

From St George turn inland through a shallow pass. From here there are good views inland to Archángelos and its castle — and over right to Moní Tsambíka. Pass a **shrine** on the right dedicated to Ágios Modéstos, one-time Bishop of Jerusalem who died in 634 AD. The shrine is most likely in memory of a local farmer, as the saint was a doctor and guardian of animals whose name day is celebrated on 16th December. The red-earth track seen ahead to the left of the castle is your eventual route. Ignore a minor track that appears to short-cut more directly to the castle; stay on the main track for another 10 minutes, then take a track off left (**2h15min**). Rise to pass well to the left of the castle, then descend to a crossing track (**2h30min**). Turn right, soon enjoying fine views over Archángelos. Take the path uphill to the right, then the steps to **Archángelos Castle** (**2h35min**).

Leave the castle via the same steps at first, but ignore the steps rising from the left used earlier. Head in the direction of the wedding-cake bell-tower. Four minutes later, cross diagonally right over a concrete track and continue downhill. Pass the church and bell-tower over to the left and descend to a T-junction. Turn right to the main road through **Archángelos**, then turn right again, back to the **bridge** (about **3h**).

STEGNA KOZAS TAVERNA
Stegná (2244 022632
**daily in season; in winter only Fri
evenings, Sat & Sun** €€

tasters include olive paste with
Archángelos village bread

various **salads**: Greek, Italian,
Cretan and the local *petroniatíki*

hearty **home-made soups** —
more than enough for a light lunch:
fish, lobster, vegetarian vegetable

meat dishes include *mousaká*
(one of the best we've ever tasted),
pastítsio, *kokkinistó*, home-made
hamburgers (can be stuffed with
féta), pork, chicken, lamb chops &
Émbonas village sausage

fresh fish in abundance daily
(unless there is no fishing due to
storms). *Rouzetiá*: a 500 g
portion of fried fish for two people,
served with a special garlic sauce

delicious **desserts** include *baklavá*, *kataïfi* with ice cream, fresh
apple pie, and yoghurt, honey &
nuts. Try one of their two special
sweets: *melekoúni* (also called
pastéli) are sesame & honey bars, a
symbol of fertility, usually made for
Greek weddings; **kserotígana**
(thiples) are deep-fried pastry
rings/shapes covered in honey,
sesame seeds and cinnamon

Kozas Taverna

Once you've sampled the food
here you'll want to return time
and again, if only to go through
as many goodies on the menu
as possible. This fish taverna is
a great favourite of the
islanders who flock here at
weekends for locally-caught
fish. Even if you aren't a fan of
fish, there is a huge choice of
dishes. Of course sometimes
not *everything* is on the menu
every day. There is also a
children's menu. Stegná Beach
was once known as 'Kozas',
which is also the family name
of the taverna owner.

restaurants
eat

To Perigiáli Taverna

A delightful find, at the opposite end of Stegná to Kozas Taverna, down by the harbour. The state-of-the-art 5-star toilets alone are worth a visit! Perigiáli is a fish taverna, but there is also grilled meat. As well as fresh fish delivered straight from

the sea onto the doorstep, there is a large selection of *mezés, perigiáli* special salad, village bread, and the best *kalamári* we've had in a long while. All washed down with an excellent house wine and just the setting to round off a good meal with a *soúma* (the local fire water), which goes well with a coffee.

TO PERIGIALI
Stegná harbour
(2244 023044
daily in season, in winter
only Fri evenings, Sat & Sun
€€

restaurants

eat

Petroniatíki salad

We have left quantities to individual taste. The salad is served in a dish for 2 persons. Toss together rocket, cherry tomatoes, chopped cucumber, chopped peppers, chopped or thinly sliced onions, black olives, *féta* cubes, oregano & mint. Top with the mashed flesh of roasted aubergine.

Petroniatíki salad at Kozas; below: *kalamári* at Taverna Oasis in Old Rhodes Town

Kalamári tiganitó (Fried squid)

Use fresh or frozen squid. Clean if necessary, then dry thoroughly. The tentacles will be separate, but leave small squid *(kalamárakia)* whole and cut large fish into rings (see photograph).

All that is needed is to coat the squid with peppered flour and fry in hot fat for about 3 min, until brown and crispy. *Overcooking toughens the flesh.* Drain on kitchen paper. Serve with lemon.

recipes

eat

Kserotígana (thiples) (Deep-fried pastry rings and shapes)

Sift the flour into a bowl. Beat the eggs and add to the flour with the lemon zest and sugar, gradually, to make a stiff dough. Add a drop of water to bind if necessary.

Knead the dough on a floured surface until it becomes smooth. Divide into 2 balls and cover with cling film (to stop it drying out while you prepare the shapes, which will be cooked in batches).

The photograph illustrates that the pastry can be prepared in various ways. You can roll out one of the balls into a long, thin strip; then, using a serrated pastry wheel, trim the edges and cut into 1.5 cm strips. Twist and twirl the strips into rings. Perhaps roll out the other ball and stamp or cut the pastry into various shapes.

Ingredients (for 4 people)

200 g self-raising flour (or use plain flour with 1 tsp of baking powder)
2 eggs
Finely grated zest of 1/2 lemon
10 g caster sugar
100 ml runny honey
chopped walnuts or sesame seeds
cinnamon
icing sugar

Shallow fry in hot oil, 3-5 cm deep, until puffed up and golden brown, turning halfway through. *Beware*: these cook in *seconds* rather than minutes!

Drain on kitchen paper, then serve sprinkled with cinnamon and/or icing sugar, drizzled with honey then topped with chopped walnuts.

Galaktoboúriko (Traditional Greek custard pie)

Custard pie is a popular sweet, with almost as many variations for the basic recipe as there are days in the month.

Prepare a dish or baking tin approximately 18 cm x 18 cm. Line the dish with 6 sheets of filo pastry. Brush each sheet with melted unsalted butter. Leave an overhang of about 4 cm.

Put the semolina, sugar and grated lemon zest (if used) in a saucepan and gradually mix in the milk. Bring to the boil, stirring constantly. Remove the pan from the heat and quickly mix in the beaten eggs. Add the vanilla essence at this stage, if you are using that instead of lemon zest. Pour the lot into the prepared baking vessel.

To make the syrup, slowly dissolve the sugar in a pan with the lemon and water, then bring to the boil. Simmer for 2 min and cool.

Top the custard with another 6 sheets of filo pastry. Tuck under the edges and brush the top with more melted butter. Score the top in a diamond or square pattern (to delineate the servings).

Bake at 180° C/gas mark 4 for 30 min, until golden brown. Then pour the cooled syrup evenly over the top and leave to soak before serving.

Ingredients (for 6 large servings)
12 sheets filo pastry
400 ml milk
60 g semolina
60 g caster sugar (Greek recipes usually call for 70 g)
2 eggs, beaten
unsalted butter, melted
1/2 lemon, finely grated zest (or 1 tsp vanilla essence if preferred)

For the syrup
130 g sugar
75 ml water
juice of 1/2 lemon

Just why this 14th-century Byzantine church is called Saint Nicholas of the Hazelnuts *(Foundoúkli)* is uncertain. The best guess is that hazel trees grew in the surrounding hills at some time in the past. Normally the church is open, so you can see the interesting old frescoes.

foundoúkli circuit

WALK

The walk starts from the church of **Ág Nikólaos Foundoúkli**; there's a shady picnic area with tables adjacent to the car park; locals sell fruit, nuts, honey and drinks here during high season. Walk along the road in the direction of Profítis Ilías. In under two minutes, turn right into a

Distance: 5km/3mi; 1h45min

Grade: moderate/strenuous, a track walk with an overall height gain of 250m/820ft; some agility required

Equipment: see page 27

Transport: 🚗 car or taxi to St Nicholas Foundoúkli. Park opposite the church.

Refreshments: café at Profítis Ilías (see Walk 7), tavernas at Apóllona; (new) Taverna Foundoúkli en route

road. The field track entering from the right almost immediately is used on the return. Pass a **ruin** on the right as the road bends left. At a junction with a **ruin** in the right-hand corner (**6min**), swing downhill to the right. (The road ahead is the return route.)

Head downhill on this road and, about six minutes from the junction, fork left downhill briefly, then ascend past olive groves. Rise onto a **ridge** (**25min**), from where there are panoramic views out to the west coast. Sálakos can be seen ahead when the far end of the ridge is reached about 10 minutes later. Start into a descent which is steep and tricky underfoot for a short section. At cross-tracks in a dip (**40min**), continue downhill to the left. There is more shade now, as the walk enters a wooded section. Two minutes along this track, fork sharp left downhill through pines, into the valley. The track curls down for 12 minutes or so, to a stream bed. Cross this, a second stream bed, and then a deeper, wider one (all three are crossed within a few minutes). This is the halfway point in the walk.

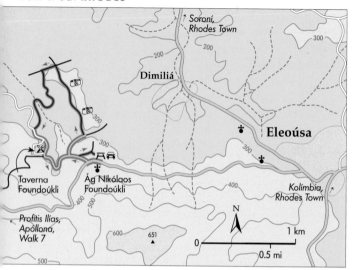

Leave the valley floor on a rough, ascending track. It bends left at first, then winds uphill to a crossing track (**1h06min**). Stay left, uphill, and soon enjoy a level section before ascending again. Pass **Taverna Foundoukli** (only open on weekends; new since our last visit and not even listed yet on trip advisor; we await your reports!). Ignore a track joining from the right (**1h06min**); keep left. Continue ahead past the road running downhill to the left (the 6min-point on the outward leg). A little further along, by a **ruin** on the left (where the road swings right to the road), take the woodland track straight ahead. As this track dips, the red dome of Ág Nikólaos Foundoúkli is seen ahead. Keep ahead in the dip, to rise through the picnic terraces to the car park at **Ág Nikólaos Foundoúkli** (**1h45min**).

Kafeneon to Elafáki, Paspallás, Panorama

Unfortunately we have not been able to check out the new Taverna Foundoúkli. If a light snack and drink are the order of the day, drive along the top road from Ág Nikólaos Foundoúkli towards Profítis Ilías, and the **Kafeneon to Elafáki** (see page 95). Or drive down to Apóllona, where there is a selection of cafés.

A more substantial repast can be had by taking the signposted road left downhill for 2.6km from the Profítis Ilías road towards Apóllona and Émbonas. At the first two T-junctions *ignore* the signposted left turns to Apóllona. (Turning left too soon,

The frescoed church of Ágios Nikólaos Foundoúkli

unless you're on foot, leads directly to the back of the village and narrow streets.) On reaching the main road (where a right turn goes to Émbonas), turn left, back towards Apóllona. Soon you will arrive at the entrance to the village and two tavernas facing each other — **Paspallás (Butcher's Taverna)**, on the right, and **Panorama Taverna** on the left (map page 94).

PASPALLAS
Apóllona, daily in season €€

specialising in **meat**, especially goat, lamb, and the local village sausage

PANORAMA
Apóllona, daily in season €€

the place to go to sample **typical village food** like *kokkinistó*, *youvétsi*, *sikóti* (liver), meat with potatoes and *mousakás*.

restaurants

eat

Soúpa revíthi (Chickpea soup) *not illustrated*

Fry the onion in the olive oil until softened, then add the garlic. Add the rest of the ingredients and bring to the boil. Cover and simmer for about 15 min, stirring occasionally.

Either leave the chickpeas whole or crush them slightly, add lemon juice and serve with the parsley garnish. (If preferred, you can thicken the soup with 1 tbsp flour mixed with the lemon juice — add this a few minutes before the end of the cooking time.)

Hint: To make this into a main meal, double all the quantities and consider adding your choice of vegetables — perhaps diced carrots, celery, mushrooms, diced courgettes or even broccoli florets.

Serve with bread and a Greek or lettuce *(maruli)* salad (see below).

<u>Ingredients (for 4 people)</u>
400 g dried chickpeas, cooked & skinned (or 2 x 400 g tins, drained)
1 onion, chopped
2 garlic cloves, crushed
2 tbsp olive oil
1 litre stock (chicken or vegetable)
1 tbsp fresh coriander, rosemary or oregano, chopped

<u>*To serve:*</u>
1 tbsp lemon juice
ground black pepper
chopped fresh parsley (garnish)
1/2 tsp cumin (optional)

Marulosaláta (Lettuce salad)

This is a very popular salad, and the herbs (especially dill) and seasoning make it very tasty.

Just cut 1 lettuce into thin strips, add 5 finely chopped spring onions and some finely chopped fresh dill (cubed cucumber can also be used if wished). Mix all these dry ingredients, then add an oil & white wine vinegar or oil & lemon dressing, season with salt and pepper and toss well.

recipes

eat

Kokkinistó (Veal or beef in tomato sauce)

Heat the butter/oil in a frying pan. Coat the meat with seasoned flour and lightly brown in the butter/oil. Add the onions and garlic, then the optional red wine (or water), cinnamon, allspice and tomatoes. Bring to the boil; then either cover the pan with a lid and simmer gently for at least two hours or pour into an ovenproof dish, cover and cook at 170° C/gas mark 3 for about 2 hours — until

the meat is tender and falling apart. This is ideal done in a slow cooker at home. Adjust the seasoning according to taste and add extra water, passata or red wine if the mixture appears too dry.

If you include carrots and celery (not Greek, but we like it!), then add more tomatoes to keep up the liquid content. (The number of fresh tomatoes used depends on the size, too — if in doubt, use more.)

Although veal or beef is used in this particular recipe, it can be made with other meat, especially chicken. The Greeks don't usually coat the meat in flour, but we prefer a thicker gravy.

Ingredients (for 4 people — generous portions)

1 kg veal or beef (cut roughly into 3 cm cubes)
100 g butter and/or oil
2 tbsp flour
2 onions, chopped
4 garlic cloves, crushed
50 ml red wine (optional) or water
1/2 tsp cinnamon
1 tsp allspice
4 large ripe tomatoes, peeled and chopped (or 1 x 400 g tin chopped tomatoes)
4 carrots, diced (optional)
2 sticks celery, chopped (optional)
salt & pepper

The charm of this walk lies in the lovely old donkey trail which climbs the hillside in long, sweeping zigzags, reaching the top with ease. Awaiting you at the top is probably one of the best dishes of yoghurt, honey and walnuts that you are likely to find on the island. The yoghurt is sourced locally and is simply the *best*.

profítis ilías from sálakos

WALK

Start the walk in **Sálakos**: leave the platia (where the tavernas are clustered) by following the road in the direction of Profítis Ilías. Pass Hotel Nymfi on the left and, as the road bends right, go left along the track signposted as a walking route to Profítis Ilías. In about two minutes, opposite a white house on the left, turn right uphill on a stony track (it may be signposted to Profítis Ilías). An imposing hillside rises ahead,

Distance: 8km/5mi; 3h

Grade: moderate-strenuous, with a climb/descent of 350m/1148ft; sometimes quite stony underfoot

Equipment: see page 27

Transport: 🚌 from Rhodes Town to Sálakos (there are a few in season; an early morning bus will allow time for the walk and a late afternoon return). 🚗 to Sálakos; park in the village — or drive the first 10 min or so of the walk and park off the motorable track near the start of the stony uphill track.

Refreshments: Sálakos tavernas, To Elafáki at Profitis Ilías (in season)

but the climb is much easier than it looks. Soon, there is a fence on your left. Just before reaching a white **shrine** on the left (**15min**), follow the fence round to the left, to continue uphill. Negotiate the animal gate in the fence, and soon start along the zigzag trail which eases your way up the very steep rock face. Some trees offer welcome shade.

You pass in front of a **water trough** on a left bend (**30min**). As the trail rises, the views are expansive and provide plenty of excuses to stop. At the **top of the trail**, the now-paved route heads towards the masts on the summit of Profítis Ilías. The trail rises again slightly, to a crossing track (**1h15min**). The onward route is to the left, but first turn right to **St Michael's church** (Ag Mixális), a fine viewpoint. The rooftops of the Hotel

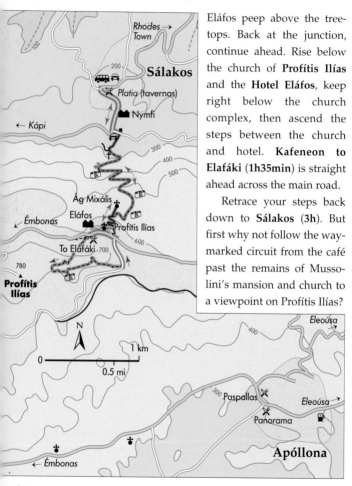

Eláfos peep above the tree-tops. Back at the junction, continue ahead. Rise below the church of **Profítis Ilías** and the **Hotel Eláfos**, keep right below the church complex, then ascend the steps between the church and hotel. **Kafeneon to Elafáki** (**1h35min**) is straight ahead across the main road.

Retrace your steps back down to **Sálakos** (**3h**). But first why not follow the way-marked circuit from the café past the remains of Mussolini's mansion and church to a viewpoint on Profítis Ilías?

Kafeneon to Elafáki

Set in the wooded slopes of Profítis Ilías on the roadside, looking down onto Hotel Eláfos, this is a pleasant spot to sit and have a drink and snack also to try a delicious yoghurt, nuts and honey.

> **KAFENEON TO ELAFAKI**
> below Profítis Ilías
> daily in season? €€
>
> various **hot and cold drinks**
>
> **ice creams**
>
> **tost** (toasted sandwiches), sandwiches, pizzas, **Greek salad**
>
> **special:** youhurt, nuts & honey

Mixális, Elefíno and Méni tavernas

Most of the tables in Sálakos square belong to **Mixális Taverna**; their menu is quite extensive and includes delicacies such as *simiakó* — small sweet shrimps from the island of Sími.

But there are two others in the square to look out for — **Taverna H Elefíno,** tucked quietly into a corner of the square and, across the road, **Taverna Méni** (next to a shop and selling local crafts).

Prices in these three tavernas are much cheaper than tavernas in more touristy areas.

restaurants

eat

Garídes tiganités (Fried prawns)

For this popular appetizer allow 100-125 g peeled king prawns per person. Coat the prawns in seasoned flour and fry in hot oil (about 5 cm deep), for not much more than 1 min. Drain on kitchen paper and serve with lemon quarters.

Hoirinó tigánia crassáta (Pork in wine sauce)

Coat the pork in the flour and brown in a pan. Remove the meat and set aside. Soften the onion in the pan, then add the oregano, cumin, wine and pork. Bring to the boil.

Reduce to a simmer and cook on a low heat, adding extra liquid (either wine or water) if required — or place in a casserole and cook at 160° C/gas mark 3 for around 1 h 30 min. (We use a slow cooker on low at home, and leave it for a few hours.)

Ingredients (for 4 people)
700 g lean pork, cubed
2 onions, chopped
400 ml white wine
2 tbsp flour, seasoned with salt & pepper
2 tsp oregano
1/2 tsp cumin

recipes
eat

Yoghurt, honey and walnuts *(karïdes)*, as served at To Elafáki

Yaoúrti me méli kai karïdes
(Yoghurt, walnuts and honey)

A quick and simple desert or snack. Buy the strained yoghurt out of a bulk container, found in larger supermarkets at the cheese and delicatessen counters, by weight (see shopping tips on page 31). Allow 150 g per person.

Stir the yoghurt well and place in individual serving dishes. Top with some honey and chopped walnuts (or your favourite nuts). This is the perfect desert with minimum effort — ideal for self catering!

97

This walk climbs through a narrow valley to emerge on stark limestone terrain populated by sparse holm oaks and a wealth of flora in early spring — including a Rhodian speciality, the red turban buttercup, *Ranunculus asiaticus*. Towards the end of the walk you enjoy an unusual — and spectacular — view of Líndos.

vlichá to líndos

WALK

Start the walk at the **bus stop**: locate the track opposite house No 613, which has large metal gates. (The building on the left-hand corner is Líndos Bay Studios, but the sign is hidden by bougainvillaea.) Initially, the track leads inland between wire fencing, into open countryside. Ignore forks to the right and stay with the track as it swings more to the left alongside **goat pens** on the left. A rusting **gravel chute** stands across the shallow gulley on the right, as the rough track heads into a narrow valley. You come to a **gate** across the track (**14min**); it may be open, but is easily bypassed in any case.

At the point where the track forks right over the stream bed (**20min**), continue ahead on a waymarked path (red dot). Stay on this path as it weaves between the rocks and rises into a **high pasture** enclosed within the hills (**30min**). Ahead, an escarpment appears to block the onward route, but cross the amphitheatre-like pasture to the right of a single, huge

Distance: 7.5km/4.7mi; 2h20min

Grade: moderate; mainly on path (waymarked) through rocky terrain and with a height gain of 170m/558ft

Equipment: see pages

Transport: 🚌 to Vlichá Bay (Rhodes/Líndos bus, departures from [2] on the plan; very frequent in the main season). Alight at the first bus stop after the Vlichá junction. Travelling by 🚗, drive downhill into Líndos and take the road heading sharp left to the beach (NB: it is easier to go round the roundabout at the bottom, in Líndos Square, and then turn *right* into this road). Park as soon as possible along this road; parking is pay-and-display, but the full-day charge is reasonable. Return to the square for a taxi and ask to be dropped by the bus stop, 1km before the Vlichá junction. This bus stop is next to the gates of house no 613.

Refreshments: plenty of choice in Líndos, and a bar/shop by the car park at the 2h10min-point

The path crosses rocky terrain at the top of the escarpment.

spreading tree at the base of the escarpment. This Valonian oak is a sheltered spot to rest and enjoy your surroundings.

Continue by following a path (marked with some cairns), towards the right-hand side of the escarpment and locate shallow **steps hewn out of the rock** (under **40min**). Climb the steps to the top of the escarpment and stay ahead as the path briefly skirts some low walls on the right. Red dots and cairns mark the route through the rocky terrain, where scattered holm oaks provide the only shade. The flora here is best in early spring, before the rocks get hot in the sun and burn up the annual flowers, bringing their season to an end.

The route heads up the valley, rising above a shallow depression on the right which falls away steeply for a while. Follow the path as it gradually crosses the top end of the depression (**50min**) and heads towards the buttress of rock at the end of the valley on the right. Reaching a high point (**1h**), descend to cross a shallow bowl, heading towards the saddle ahead. The rock buttress is to the right. Reach the **saddle** (**1h10min**) and pass through a gap in the wall, to descend through the rocks. Views open up — to the sea and abandoned terraces on the plateau below. The path continues towards the plateau but veers left, contouring, just before it's reached. Soon, the path skims very close to the **cliff edge** (**1h20min**) above the Líndos/Péfkos road. Suddenly, the land drops away (**1h35min**), to reveal a stunning view of Líndos acropolis ahead.

Follow the path carefully downhill to a tarmac road and turn left. You reach the large **car park** above Líndos near Super Market Flora over to the left (**2h10min**). To reach the village, cross the road diagonally left and take the narrow main road downhill. Or turn right along the road briefly, pass a fenced compound on the left, then take a path off left (where Líndos View Hotel is on the right). This path meets another path behind the compound; turn right here, then follow a steep path and steps cut into the side of the cliffs downhill into **Líndos village** (**2h20min**).

Maria's Taverna

A plethora of tavernas confronts visitors to Líndos, some good, some indifferent. Maria's is worth seeking out: from the main square follow signs to the Acropolis. When you reach the Church of the Panagía, with tower and courtyard on the left, turn right. This street leads through Líndos to St Paul's Bay. At a right/left kink in the street, turn down the street on the left; Maria's is just on the right. Very good air conditioning and an excellent menu compensate for the lack of an outside area.

A short distance further along the street towards St Paul's Bay is **Arxondíko**, an up-market (dinner only) restaurant in an old Lindian mansion, with a roof-top terrace — ideal for special occasions (€€€).

Mythos (€€) is but one of many similar Líndos tavernas, but with quite a good menu and an excellent view over the village towards the sea and the Acropolis. To locate it, leave the main square by the road uphill to the right, alongside the donkey station; Mythos is then on the right. Many Greek specialities, including *kléftiko*, *youvétsi*, *stifádo*, *mousaká* and grills.

> **MARIA'S TAVERNA**
> **Líndos (2244 031375**
> **daily 10.00–24.00 €€**
>
> A chance to try Lindian shrimp risotto (same as the small, sweet Sími shrimps), avocado with honey and walnuts, and *bouyoúrdi* (a local name for *saganáki sto foúrno*), plus the special of the day, etc. A good cold CAIR retsína goes especially well with lunch.

restaurants

eat

Garíthes piláfi (Shrimp risotto)

Although this photograph shows Maria's small sweet Sími shrimps, shrimp risotto was the dish of the day when we were last there. It's very

tasty and easily made with pre-cooked and peeled shrimps — a great meal in one pot.

There are choices to make. Whole unpeeled fresh prawns add more flavour but can be messy to eat — more fun, but have plenty of napkins to hand. Or use fresh prawns/shrimps and peel before cooking, then strain the liquid and use it to cook the rice. Or buy ready-cooked, to save on the preparation.

Heat the oil in a large pan and cook the onions and garlic until they are translucent. Add the peppers, mushrooms and celery and cook until softened. Add the tomatoes and seasonings and cook gently for about 10 min, then add the rice and *uncooked* prawns/shrimps. (Add ready-cooked just before the rice is done.)

Stir well and simmer for 15 min. Keep an eye on the liquid, adding water as necessary, until it's absorbed and the rice is cooked. If using cooked prawns/shrimps, add to the mixture just before the rice is ready, then the optional crumbled *féta* cheese and/or peas.

Ingredients (for 4 people)

500 g prawns/shrimps, rinsed and cleaned, or 400 g already peeled and cooked
3 tbsp olive oil
1 small onion, chopped
1 garlic clove, crushed
1 large red pepper, chopped
200 g button mushrooms, whole
2 sticks celery, chopped (optional)
400 g tin chopped tomatoes
1/2 tsp oregano
salt & pepper
200–300 g long grain rice
100 g crumbled *féta* cheese (optional)
100 g fresh (cooked) or frozen peas (optional)

Melizanosaláta (Roasted aubergine dip) *not illustrated*

This dish is a popular *mezé* starter. Wrap a couple of aubergines in foil and bake in the oven at 180° C/gas mark 4 for an hour or more, until *very* soft. (To get the distinctive smoky flavour of an authentic *saláta*, the aubergines must be cooked on a barbecue.) Scoop out the flesh and beat until smooth. Add seasonings to taste: garlic (mashed to a creamy paste), then olive oil, lemon, salt & pepper. The finished mix should be firm and not sloppy.

Kolokithákia tiganitá (Fried courgettes)

Another great *mezé* starter; we're always asking for them, even if they're not on the menu! Really quick and easy to prepare, but they need to be eaten *immediately*.

Top and tail washed courgettes, then slice into thin rings. (If using small or baby courgettes, slice them lengthwise, as in the photograph.) Dust in seasoned flour and fry in about 5 cm of hot oil until browned. Drain on kitchen paper and serve at once.

Courgette flowers (shown above) are also delicious battered and fried — they can be stuffed with *féta*.

Ingredients (for 4 people)
0.5 kg courgettes
seasoned flour
oil for frying

recipes
eat

There are many variations on the **mousakás** theme, but all basically contain the same ingredients. It's a matter of personal taste how you put them together. Some recipes use only aubergines; others (including ours), potato. Anything goes; it depends a great deal on the flavouring.

This is an easy recipe to adjust for any number of people. Even the topping can be a straightforward cheese sauce, béchamel, or one containing egg yolk. We use the béchamel option in this recipe, but it's worth experimenting with the different options.

Frying the aubergines and potatoes can turn this into a very oily (but very tasty) dish. But the aubergine slices can be brushed with oil and baked or dry-fried. Our long-used method is to layer the aubergine (1 cm thick slices) in a dish, drizzling a little oil over each layer: cover with clingfilm and microwave until soft, around 8-10min. Halve the potatoes and boil them until almost cooked.

Mousakás (Moussaka)

Pre-cook the aubergines and potatoes as above. Heat some oil in a frying pan and gently stir-fry the onions and garlic to soften. Add the meat and brown, still stirring. Drain off any excess fat/liquid. Now add the herbs, spices, and salt & pepper to taste. Moisten with the tomato juice if using tinned. Grease a 2.5 l ovenproof dish or large casserole.

Place a layer of aubergine slices in the base of the dish, then the meat. Top with a further layer of aubergine slices and the chopped tomatoes. Finally, place a layer of sliced potatoes on the top.

For the sauce, make a roux with the flour and butter by melting the butter and combining with the flour then, using a balloon whisk, gradually add the milk and seasoning. Continue to stir over the heat until the mixture boils and thickens. (If using a microwave, melt the butter, then add the flour using a balloon whisk to combine the two, and microwave on high for 40 seconds. Gradually whisk in the milk and seasoning. Microwave on high for 2 min, stir, then continue in

1 min bursts, stirring in between, until the sauce bubbles and thickens. Watch carefully, to prevent the mixture boiling over.)

Spread the sauce over the mixture in the dish, sprinkle over some grated cheese and bake at 180° C/gas mark 4 for 30-40 min, until brown on top.

The *mousaká* can be frozen for a few weeks or left overnight on the chiller tray in the fridge, which will enhance the flavour.

Alternative vegetarian version: Replace the meat with about 100 g of cooked puy or green lentils and a mixture of sliced vegetables. For example, heat some olive oil and butter in a frying pan, soften 2 onions, then add 2 sliced carrots, 2 sliced sticks of celery, 4 large chopped tomatoes (or a 400 g tin of tomatoes), a handful of fresh parsley, salt & pepper and an optional dash of red or white wine. Simmer for around 30 min, then add the cooked lentils. Use as the meat layer in the main dish.

Alternative topping: Use the basic sauce recipe above, seasoned with salt & pepper, then stir in 1 egg yolk and 60 g of grated cheese.

Ingredients (for 6 people)
500 g lamb or beef, minced
2-3 pre-cooked aubergines (1 kilo)
2 pre-cooked medium potatoes
2 medium onions, chopped
3 garlic cloves, crushed
1 tin (400 g) plum (or chopped) tomatoes, or 4 large ripe tomatoes, skinned & chopped
1 tsp basil
1 tsp oregano
1 tsp allspice
salt & pepper to taste
olive or other oil (to drizzle over the aubergines and for frying)
For the sauce:
600 ml warmed milk
2 tbsp flour
60 g butter
1/2 tsp nutmeg
2 bay leaves
ground black pepper

Mount Akramítis, the second-highest mountain on Rhodes, peaks at 823m/2700ft, topping Profítis Ilías (Walk 7) by 43m. We climb to the tiny wilderness church of Ág Ioánnes and return the same way. Farm ruins and deserted fields lie en route, now abandoned for easier living elsewhere, and the mountain is left to walkers.

mount akramítis

WALK

The walk begins at the **lay-by on the east side of the Siána road,** 0.9 km northeast of Monolíthos. The path is on the opposite side of the road and marked by **yellow-painted cairns**. Clamber up the bank, then between the cairns and head into the woods. In under two minutes, watch for the onward path turning sharply left uphill (waymarks and cairns). Later (**15min**), the main route forks right to continue uphill. (The path ahead at this point leads to an excellent viewpoint in under 20min.) The climb is steep, but cypress trees provide some

Distance: 8.6km/5.4mi; 3h

Grade: strenuous, with an ascent/ descent of 340m/1115ft. There is a constant pull uphill for the first 30min, with a steep and stony section between the 10min- and 20min-points.

Equipment: see page 27; plenty of water

Transport: There is no convenient bus to Monolíthos. �'take a taxi to Monolíthos, and either alight by Christós Corner Taverna and walk 15min uphill along the road towards Siána to the start of the walk, or ask the driver to drop you 0.9 km along the Siána road from Monolíthos, by a lay-by on the right (this is where you should park if you come by car).

Refreshments: Christós Corner Taverna at the road junction in Monolíthos; none en route

shade and viewpoints a good excuse to stop. The trail/path has clearly long been an old route up to the pastures cradled within the mountain range, as retaining walls indicate.

The path levels out for a short distance as you enter the **pine tree belt** (**45min**). Reach a **clearing** (**1h**) and cross diagonally right, to exit at '2 o'clock'. A good few minutes later you descend into the bowl of a valley. The path stays mostly to the left side and, after passing a **ruin** on the left, rises at the far end of the valley into a smaller abandoned field. Rise again, through a **gap in a wall** (**1h15min**), into a large flat area. Another slight rise a few minutes later sees the route heading directly towards a sheer rock face. Under 15 minutes later (**1h30min**), look for a **blue arrow and blue dots** indicating a path uphill to the right. (Blue marks usually indicate the route to a church.) Turn right here and carefully follow cairns and blue dots in a rocky ascent.

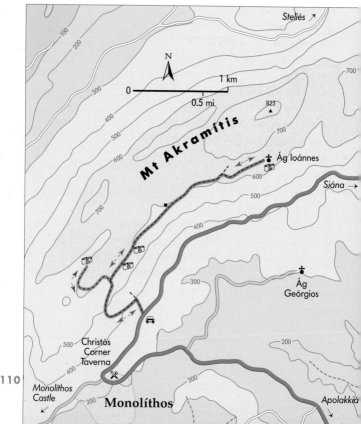

As the climb lessens, follow the waymarked path towards the church, surrounded by a walled compound, now in view ahead. Clamber over a wooden barrier to keep out goats (watch out for nails!). Inside the compound (actually a water cistern) you come to tiny **Ág Ioánnes** (**1h40min**). This 800-year-old church has long been a shelter and water source for the local goatherds and farmers. Set high amidst a rocky wilderness, this is a peaceful place just to soak in the atmosphere and admire the views, but don't drink the water from the well in the courtyard!

On the ascent to Ág Ioánnes

Return the same way, following the waymarks and cairns back downhill to the **lay-by on the Siána road** (**3h**). You enjoy a completely different perspective on the descent. Those with energy to spare can divert right to the viewpoint mentioned at the 10min-point on the ascent (allow an extra 35min).

Christós Corner Taverna

A taverna commanding an excellent elevated location, at the road junction in Monolíthos, Christós Corner offers a delicious choice of Greek cuisine. Our readers love it! There is a huge selection of *mezédes* to sample before you even make a start on the specialities and grills. You could be there for hours — everything is so tasty, including the house wine. Their *gígantes* are among the best we've ever tasted. Ingredients are fresh and mostly local produce. Easy to make, *tirokeftédes* are always tucked into with relish. See recipe and photo opposite, ingredients below:

> **CHRISTOS CORNER TAVERNA**
> **Monolíthos daily in season** €€
>
> very wide menu; some **highlights** include:
>
> *bakaliáraki tiganitó* (fried cod balls)
>
> *tirokeftédes* (cheese balls)
>
> *melitzanosaláta* (aubergine dip)
>
> omelettes, salads, *mousakás*
>
> **charcoal grilled specialities**: lamb, goat and special village sausage
>
> house **dry white wine** excellent, with a hint of muscat

Tirokeftédes: ingredients (for 20 cheese balls)
300 g grated hard cheese (gouda, *kasseri, regato,* etc, or cheddar)
60 g SR flour (or plain with 1/2 tsp baking powder)
2 eggs

restaurants

eat

Gígantes (Giant butter beans in sauce)

Soak the beans in plenty of water overnight. Strain, then cover with water again and boil gently for about 40 min. Don't overcook the beans; they need to be *just* cooked without being too soft.

Mix together all the other ingredients, stir in the beans, then place in a greased tin or dish and cover with foil. Bake at 200° C/gas mark 6 for 30-40 min. Check towards the end of the cooking time, and add extra water/ tomato juice and/or seasoning if necessary. Serve hot or cold — as a starter or as a vegetable.

Tirokeftédes (Cheese balls)

Beat the eggs and combine with the other ingredients *(listed opposite)*. Roll pieces of the mixture into small walnut-sized balls. Dust lightly with flour and fry in very hot oil, enough to cover, for a just few minutes.

<u>Ingredients (for 6 people, as a starter)</u>

250 g dried butter beans (or 3 x 400 g tins)

2 garlic cloves, crushed

100 ml olive oil

3 large ripe tomatoes, skinned & chopped (or 1 x 400 g tin of chopped tomatoes)

1 small onion, chopped

1 tsp dried parsley or 1 heaped tbsp of fresh flat-leaved parsley, shredded

2 level tsp cumin

salt & pepper to taste

Optional: chopped carrot and celery can be added to the mix, and curry powder instead of cumin also works quite well

recipes

eat

This compact walk is full of interesting features. We start at Kritinía Castle, with fine views. Our descent through a gorge is spectacular — and easy into the bargain. An ancient temple awaits by the shore; neglected and forlorn, it feels like a personal discovery. The return to the castle is amazingly direct, straight up the hillside.

kritinía castle

WALK

Kritinía Castle was originally built by the Knights of St John on three levels; each level was assigned to a different Grand Master. Apart from remnants of the chapel, there is little to see inside. **The walk begins** at the T-junction just downhill from the castle, where you turn right (south) on the track. In three minutes, meet cross-tracks and turn left. (The return route enters from the right here.) Ignore a track forking left but, seven minutes from the cross-tracks, as the main track makes a U-bend to the left, go right down the rough wide track (you may spot a few red waymarks). This track may have been ploughed over, in which case just head down the left-hand side for a few minutes. When the track ends, continue ahead on a path around the contour of the hill.

On meeting a crossing

Distance: 4km/2.5mi; 1h30min

Grade: moderate, on tracks and paths (with a very slight possibility of vertigo in a part of the gorge section). The altitude gain from sea level back to the castle is 130m/430ft. Prickly shrubs are invasive in places, so wear long trousers and long sleeves.

Transport: 🚗 taxi (arrange to be collected again) or car to Kritinía Castle and back. Park anywhere nearby. *Be aware* of the two ladies, one on the road up to the castle, the other opposite the castle, who accost the unwary traveller during the tourist season. The first one thrusts a note into your hand which declares: 'I am the keeper of the castle, and I'm responsible for keeping it clean and tidy and I do not get paid.' The second demands €1 for parking up at the castle. They're both neat little income-generators, and there's no reason to feel you have to comply!

Refreshments: choice of tavernas in Kámiros Skála and in Kámiros. The elevated *platia* in Kámiros is another pleasant place to linger and enjoy the view over the countryside. Kafeneon O Plátanos and café/restaurant H Riatsa in the *platia* both serve Greek specialities. There is a café at Kritinía Castle, but nothing en route.

Hálki

Cape Kopriá

Taverna
Althemenis

Rhodes Town

Kámiros Scála

Kritinía
Castle Café

Tennis

Kritinía

Platia
Kafenion Platanos
H Riatza Taverna

N

0   1 km

0.5 mi

Monolithos

track, stay downhill to the right, descending steadily towards the **gorge**. As this track ends, keep ahead along the edge of a field on the left for half a minute, then continue ahead on a red-waymarked path (**25min**). Ignore a downhill path almost at once, and stay alongside a **wall** on the right. The path edges the side of the gorge on the left and may be slightly vertiginous in places. Soon views open up to the sea ahead through the V of the gorge. As the path descends to the bottom of the valley (**45min**), stay on the path to the right, with a **wire fence** to your left. You reach the shore at an **ancient temple** (**50min**); partly excavated, it has been abandoned to the elements.

To return, go right around the end of the fence (taking care at the edge of the cliff), and follow the path uphill *(not way-marked)*. The path initially parallels the coast more or less, but after several minutes it heads more inland. Ascend through a rock channel (**1h05min**), to where a **wire fence** blocks the way ahead. (Originally, the route went to the left, but a fence has been erected along the path, and the way is now blocked.) Continue to wind up to the left, to the top of the hill — where the castle is in view ahead. Heading towards the castle, make for the left-hand side of a structure visible ahead, downhill, through the trees. When you get there (it turns out to be a **tennis court**), aim for the right-hand corner and the start of a field track. Follow this track alongside the tennis court (now on your left), to a crossing track (**1h20min**). Turn left towards the castle and ignore a track off left. Rise to meet the outward cross-tracks (**1h25min**) and continue left uphill, back to **Kritinía Castle** (**1h30min**) — where the café may be a welcome sight…

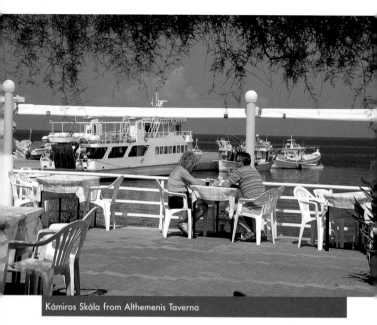

Kámiros Skála from Althemenis Taverna

Kámiros Skála is usually a peaceful backwater. Most of the activity revolves around the arrival of the ferry from Hálki and local fishing boats. It can be quite interesting when a boat load of sheep arrives and they have to be transferred onto the quay! For the most part though, the only sound is the gentle whooshing of waves on the shingle and muted conversation.

restaurants
eat

Althemenis Taverna

Three tavernas beckon at Kámiros Skála. The one opposite the entrance to the harbour usually has a lone male figure, probably grandad, standing in wait trying to entice passing motorists inside. If this doesn't appeal, turn into the harbour road and park in the car park on the left. There is a pleasant taverna in a corner beyond this car park, but Althemenis (fish taverna) has the *best* position, by the water.

> **ALTHEMENIS TAVERNA**
> **Kámiros Skála**
> **open daily in season** €€
> **English menu available**
>
> large selection of **mezés**, and Sími shrimps feature — as well as yummy *tirokeftédes* (cheese balls)
>
> the **speciality is fish**, and *skordaliá* (garlic dip) is an essential accompaniment to fish here, even with *kolokithákia* (fried courgette)
>
> limited choice of **meat** dishes

The prices, in kilos for fish, are quite good, and the menu as a whole extensive. (See page 12 about ordering fish by weight.) The seal of approval regarding its popularity is the number of Greek clients, especially at weekends and holidays.

If on the other hand you are driving to Rhodes Town from Kritinía and are looking for a place en route, try **Taverna Akrogiáli** at the Kritinía end of Kalavárda. We often stop off here, to enjoy the ambience. Choose from traditional Greek fare and fish. It's a typical Greek fish taverna on the edge of the shore, with a cameo view overlooking a small sandy beach with fishing boats and tamarisk trees.

Along the same road, note **Taverna Koúfas**, across the road from the airport. We haven't eaten there yet, but it could be an excellent fall-back for those whose flights are held up for an hour or two — an excellent escape from the confines of a hot (and probably overcrowded) airport.

Marídes tiganités (Fried whitebait)

Fish like *marídes* and *atherina* are eaten whole and go well with oúzo. These are easy to cope with if self-catering. When buying, the smaller the fish the better. This method also works well at home with whitebait. Allow about 200 g of small fish per person. If serving as a *mezé*, the quantity will depend on how many other dishes are offered.

Wash and dry the fish and coat with seasoned flour, shaking off excess flour. Heat some light oil (*not* olive oil) in a deep pan (fill to a depth of at least 5 cm), until very hot. Fry the fish in the hot oil until brown — which won't take long. Drain on kitchen paper and serve with lemon quarters.

Skordaliá (Garlic dip) *not illustrated*

A very popular sauce on Rhodes — and easy to make. Traditionally served with fish, it also goes well with beetroot and *hórta* (see page 14).

Boil the potatoes in their skins. When cool, discard the skins and mash well. Add the garlic paste a little at a time, until you achieve the strength you want.

Gradually blend in the olive oil, vinegar and salt & pepper, until the mixture is creamy (but not sloppy) and to the required taste.

Ingredients (for 4 people)
450 g large floury potatoes
8 garlic cloves, mashed into a
  creamy paste
50 ml olive oil
25 ml white wine vinegar
salt & pepper

recipes

eat

Horiátiki saláta (Greek salad)

Traditionally made *without* lettuce, this salad comes in many variations. It can be served with sliced lettuce or sliced white cabbage (usually when fresh lettuce isn't easily available). The lettuce or cabbage is placed in the base of the serving dish and the other ingredients layered on the top. Alternatively, the ingredients are tossed together with cubed *féta* cheese. Anything goes!

Greek salad at Christós Corner (Walk 9), with shredded white cabbage below the *féta*, and pickled chillis adding a final touch

Place the ingredients in a serving dish as shown here, with slabs of *féta* cheese on top. Olive oil is drizzled on the *féta*, along with a sprinkling of dried oregano.

Angourodomáto saláta (Tomato & cucumber salad)

This simple salad is very tasty when you want something light. The tomatoes and cucumber are sliced and drizzled with olive oil, then sprinkled with oregano and salt. Thinly sliced onion can also be included.

Ingredients (for 4 people)

1 fresh lettuce, washed and shredded
3 tomatoes, cut into wedges
1/2 cucumber, sliced or cubed
1 onion, finely sliced
1 green pepper, finely sliced
black olives to taste
250 g *féta* cheese, in thick slices
olive oil & vinegar or lemon
dried oregano & dill (but fresh dill makes this salad really tasty)
salt & pepper

121

One of the most beautiful places in the Mediterranean, you just cannot go to Rhodes without visiting Líndos. Almost everybody does so by joining an organised coach tour. *Do* take our advice and plan your own tour, to escape the crowds. Perhaps combine it with the short walk described on page 127.

líndos

EXCURSION

Dozens of coaches arrive at Líndos during the morning, pouring out visitors by the hundreds. All of them tread the same path up through the narrow streets, then swarm over the acropolis. The normal itinerary then is back to the coach and leave — or lunch, then leave.

So devise your own tour! Visitor numbers to the acropolis tend to reduce markedly by 3pm, so the best plan is to have lunch before climbing up to explore it. There is plenty to fill the morning. Curving around the bay and overlooked by the acropolis is a large beach of fine golden sand with plenty of facilities. If you prefer a little more solitude, try the engaging short walk out to the tomb of Kleoboulos described on page 127. It's on the northern tip of the bay and will give you a wholly different perspective on Líndos.

Description: allow a full day, to take in the sights, have lunch, and do the short walk described on page 127

Transport: 🚌 or 🚗 to Líndos (as Walk 8, page 99). Parking is not a problem if you drive along the beach-side road looking for a metered space or keep going, because there is field parking further on, up the left fork on the sweeping bend (see map on page 100). The further you go, the easier it is to find parking, and it's particularly handy for the beach.

Refreshments: cafés, fast-food outlets, tavernas and restaurants abound in Líndos; see Walk 8.

Overview of Excursions 1 and 2

Tourist shops, coffee bars, and fast-food outlets pack the narrow, winding, climbing streets of the village. Little churches

123

are tucked away in these streets, too, and some fine old traditional houses built by wealthy ship-owners in the 17th to 19th centuries. Except for a high ornate wall and a heavily decorated door there is little to see but, occasionally, a door is left ajar. A glimpse through the doorway reveals a flower-filled courtyard with a floor of decorative pebbles. Black and white pebbles are favoured and used rather like a Roman mosaic to make a design or motif. This style of pebble floors, known as *hockláki*, is popular on Rhodes and widely used. Unfortunately, these traditional *arxondíko* houses are diminishing, many being converted into restaurants and shops.

If you wander the streets, keeping inland of the acropolis hill, you can easily reach St Paul's Bay on the south side of the town. Just keep the acropolis to the left as you meander through the narrow streets and, when you get a more open view, you can see the remains of an ancient theatre below the acropolis.

The small, almost land-locked bay of St Paul's does have a small beach, and development is taking place there slowly but steadily (there is also plenty of car parking space). St Paul visited Rhodes on his way from Miletus to Syria to help convert the island to Christianity, and it's believed he landed here. The small church tucked away on the far side of the bay is dedicated to him.

If you don't want to struggle up the hill to the acropolis, you can take the romantic option and travel by donkey to the castle, pretending you are a knight on horseback. By the afternoon many of the lace-sellers lining the route have lost their appetite for pressing tourists to buy their beautiful work. Some of it is made by hand by the local ladies over the winter months, but imports have added volume and variety.

When you have finally climbed 116m/380ft, almost to the top of this flat-topped outcrop of rock, you reach the pay booth. Too late now to change your mind!

Location is everything, and this huge rock defends two natural harbours which has made it a desirable residence ever since man first formed settlements. Occupation can be traced back to the Neolithic Age (2500-2000 BC), but it was not until around the 10th century BC that Líndos really rose to prominence — along with two other cities of antiquity on the island, Kámiros and Ialyssós. A temple dedicated to Athena Líndos has existed on this rock from at least that period.

Kleoboulos, who governed the city for 40 years in the 6th century BC, ruled moderately and wisely and drew great respect from all over Greece. He was one of the 'Seven Sages' of Ancient Greece. By this time Líndos had become a great maritime trading city and had extended its trade zone to include Egypt, Cyprus and Syria. With the growing stature of the city, Kleoboulos improved the sanctuary to Athena by building a larger temple, thought to have had a four-columned portico at each end but without columns along the sides. The archaic staircase seen below the modern one may also be his contribution.

Around 342 BC the temple built by Kleoboulos burnt down, together with the statue of Athena and many of the votive offerings. The Lindians promptly built a new one in its place, repeating the original style, but with an even bigger statue showing Athena standing and not seated as in the original. The statue this time was built with a body of gold-plated wood and limbs of marble.

Later, in the Hellenistic Period around 200 BC, further developments took place on the acropolis, which brought it to its final form. A huge double-winged covered colonnade, a *stoa*, was added on the north side, embracing the steps up to the propylaeum and covering the whole width of the entrance. A small temple built in the northwest corner is thought to be Roman. On the western outer flank of the acropolis is a 4th-century BC theatre cut into the rock, with 27 rows of seats still preserved. If you did not see this walking over to St Paul's Bay, you can get a good view looking over the walls. Also outside the acropolis and near the theatre are the foundations of ancient walls believed to have formed part of a gymnasium.

View from the acropolis across Lindos Bay towards the Kleoboulos Tomb (behind the left-hand column)

The present fortifications are the work of the Knights of St John who, in the Byzantine era, remodelled and strengthened the walls of an earlier fortification. Restoration is a permanent feature these days — so expect scaffolding.

Tomb of Kleoboulos

Start the walk from the **main square in Líndos**: walk uphill, as if leaving the village, then turn right on the road to the beach. As this bends right five minutes later, ascend the narrow tarmac road on the left signposted to the Tomb of Kleoboulos. At the entrance to a field (used as a car park), go along the walled-in path to the left of the gateway. The path soon leaves the walls behind and emerges in a very stony landscape. In around 10 minutes, you come to a **memorial** to a long-serving local politician who hailed from Líndos.

See map on page 100
Distance: 5.6km/3.5mi; 1h35min
Grade: easy, waymarked path, with a short climb to the tomb
Equipment: see page 27
Transport, Refreshments: as Walk 8, page 98

Windmill en route to the Tomb of Kleoboulos; take care if you go inside!

Over to the right is Líndos, and ahead is the rotunda (tomb), at the end of the promontory. The path skirts to the left of a deep inlet, then heads through a gap in the wall to the **windmill** shown above (**35min**). Beware of the dangerous state of the interior if venturing inside. Pick up the path again behind the windmill and skirt another smaller inlet. Cairns guide the way through the rocks as the path ascends a rocky outcrop to the **Tomb of Kleoboulos** (**50min**); see history, see pages 126-127.

Return the same way.

There is a huge choice of sailings from Rhodes to different islands. We have chosen Kastellórizo, the most easterly island in Greece. Although it lies a fair distance away (72 nautical miles and very close to Kaş in Turkey), the journey by fast catamaran only takes about 2h30min, leaving five hours to explore.

kastellórizo

EXCURSION

Kastellórizo is the modern name for the island, which was called Megísti in ancient times. Legend tells that Megisthus, a Cretan prince, was the first settler and named the island after himself. Perhaps less romantic is the suggestion that the name arose because it's largest of all the fourteen small islands spread around the area. The present name came into use during the Crusades as a

Description: a full day out, with 5h on board the catamaran and 5h to explore Kastellórizo; *see overview map on page 123*

Transport: ⛴ from Rhodes Town (departures from V on the plan on pages 38-39). Cost about €40. It's windy on deck travelling at speed, but there is plenty of inside cabin space for both smokers and non-smokers, and the journey is smooth enough usually to settle into a good book.

Refreshments: ample cafés, tavernas and restaurants; for our suggestion see page 135.

corruption of 'Kastel Roso', the name of the castle built from the island's red rocks. Five hours ashore is perfect for this picturesque tiny island, just 9 sq km (3.5 sq mi), with less than 300 hundred inhabitants. It leaves enough time to explore the main town by taking the short walk outlined on the following pages and then enjoy a good lunch.

Like many Greek islands, Kastellórizo has had a chequered history. There are footsteps of the Minoans and Myceneans from early times and, later, the Romans, Lycians, Greeks, Egyptians, Turks, Venetians, French and Italians. Now it's administered from Rhodes.

The island came under Turkish rule in 1537 and, granted special trading privileges, it flourished for a time. During the 19th century the population had increased to 9000 inhabitants, supported by a good trade from sponge fishing. It was in this period of wealth that many of its churches and fine houses were built.

Kastellórizo entered a period of turbulence as it tried to break free from the Turks. In its final attempt, the uprising was put down by France (as an ally of Italy); France then used the island as a base for operations against Syria. In the First World War Kastellórizo was bombarded from the Turkish coast. Italy took control in 1921, restricted trade, and tried to de-Hellenise the island. Damage caused by the earthquake of 1927 was not repaired by the Italians, and the island's prosperity declined further, with many starting to emigrate. By 1940 the population was estimated to be around 1400. When the Italians surrendered in 1943, freedom appeared to be in sight when the British arrived, but the island continued to suffer severe bombing raids from the Germans. Eventually, in 1947, it was reunited with Greece — but not before yet more of the populace had left for a life elsewhere.

There are many stories to tell of the thousands who left Kastellórizo, principally for Australia, to find work and start again. Lots of these 'Kassies', as they call themselves, are still proud of their island and have returned to reclaim and renovate their old homes, but few remain as permanent residents.

A first surprise on entering the harbour is the rather striking Turkish mosque and minaret on the headland, but your first impression may be just how serene this rocky island looks. Colourful houses interspersed with shops and tavernas ribbon the deep, natural harbour — all guarded by the remains of a

Crusader castle on the hill above the mosque. This port town, **Megísti**, is the largest on the island and is split into two parts, Pigádia around the port, and Horáfia over the hill beyond the castle. The walk described below takes a look at both parts. If you just prefer

Distance: 5km/3mi; allow 2h

Grade: easy, although there are plenty of steps (ascending about 100m/300ft overall)

Equipment: good walking shoes, ample water

Refreshments: only at the start and finish

to relax, stop at the Megísti Hotel, where there is an attractive terrace with sun beds for hire. The water in the harbour sparkles with clarity and is good for swimming or snorkelling.

Our walking tour never strays too far from the port where the boat awaits your return so, if you feel time is running away, there is always a direct route back. Although this ranks little more than a stroll, it's packed with interest, including the mosque, museum, castle, windmill and Lycian tomb.

Turn right on leaving the boat, and walk all the way around the **harbour square** to the **Megísti Hotel** at the furthest point. On the way you pass a church with a clock tower: look out here for the **Akrothalassi Taverna**, our suggestion for lunch. Turn around at the hotel and walk back the same way, to get a different view of the harbour and to start the walk below.

Walking tour of Megísti

Start the walk at the **church with the clock tower**: turn right here, to walk down its left side; go left, then right, to find the church of **St George of the Rock**. Return to the harbourside to

131

Megísti
(not to scale)

Hotel
Megísti

Limáni

Pigádia

Agorá
(Market)

Horáfia

Mandráki

1 Clock tower church
2 St George of the Rock
3 Taverna Akrothalassi
4 Taverna Lazaraki
5 Taverna Athena
6 Customs House
7 Mosque
8 Museum
9 St Dimítri & St Nicholas
10 Castle
11 Windmill
12 St Constantine & Eléni
13 Ág Spiridon & Lady Panagía
14 St George's
15 Desalination plant
16 Lycian rock tomb
17 Jetty

continue, and notice the old *agorá*, the **market** building. Walking the final straight side of the harbour, it's easy to pick out the mosque, castle and windmill which line the ongoing route.

Nearing the end of the harbour, go right alongside the **Customs House**, with the **mosque** now on your left. Climb the steps to arrive at the **museum** (07.00-14.00; cl Mon) and walk along the front of it, with the museum on your left. The route now heads above and parallel with the port (*limáni*), so there are good views down over it. At a T-junction of more major steps, turn left uphill, quickly reaching the twin churches of **Ág Nikólaos** and **Ág Dimítri** on the left. Just beyond are the remains of a **castle** restored by the Knights of St John in 1309. Steps take you up the remains and a vertical iron ladder completes the ascent. From the top you can appreciate the twin nature of the churches when you see the two adjacent barrel-vaulted roofs and enjoy a view of the scattered islands and the Turkish mainland.

A paved path complete with lamp posts leads from the castle towards Horáfia, passing the old **windmill** on the way. A few minutes later you reach a road and enter a huge square with a school and churches. This is Horáfia. The important church to see here is **St Constantine and Eléni**, on the left (within the school complex), built in 1835 of granite from the temple of Apollo brought from Patara in Turkey. Possibly only Sunday and Holy Day visitors will find it open. Still on the left there are two churches together, **Our Lady Panagía** and, set back a little, the smaller **Ág Spirídon**. The huge twin-towered church opposite, on the far side of the square, is **St George's**, built in 1903 on the remains of an earlier church. In the middle is a monument to Despiná Achladiotou, a remarkable lady who lived to a ripe old age. She is remembered for her defiance in resisting evacuation during World War II, raising the Greek flag each day and co-operating with the allies.

Turn left out of the square to follow the road downhill towards the seafront, passing the schoolyard on the left. At the bottom, first turn left behind the houses, then continue almost immediately to the coast and up the gravel drive leading towards a house. Before reaching the house, take the footpath which continues to follow the shore for a short while, before turning down paved steps and meeting steps downhill opposite (coming from between the castle and windmill). There is a small church on the left here, as well as the island's desalination plant.

Turn right and follow the paved walkway around the coast back towards the harbour. If you can take your eyes away from the seascape with the offshore islands, watch out for the sign on the left to the **Lycian tomb**. There are yet more steps to climb, but the tomb is a fine, undamaged example and worth seeing. Return to the path and follow it to the **mosque** on the headland, passed on the outward route. The **harbour** is now just ahead.

Taverna Akrothalassi

We chose this waterside taverna as a pleasant retreat from the main activity and bustle of the harbour. The food is good and freshly prepared. For those wanting to be more into quayside activity, **Tavernas Athena** and **Lazaráki** sit side by side further along the harbour, in the centre.

Akrothalassi has a fairly traditional menu (€€), with a mix of meat and fish dishes. Their stuffed peppers and tomatoes are especially tasty.

restaurants

eat

Spanakópita (Spinach pie)

Wash the spinach well, dry it, trim off thick stems, and shred. Heat the oil in a frying pan and cook the onion, garlic, spring onions (and leek, if used) until soft. Add the herbs, then the spinach, and toss the mixture until the spinach wilts and excess moisture evaporates.

Stir in the féta and add pepper and salt to taste. Remember, the cheese will be fairly salty. (Lancashire creamy or crumbly cheese — even mixed with grated cheddar — make good substitutes for *féta*.)

Prepare a 26 cm x 20 cm oblong dish or tin (like a large lasagne dish) or 20 cm round dish or tin and lightly oil. Roll out your pastry of choice, or butter and layer about 5 sheets of filo pastry, and line the dish or tin.

Fill with the spinach and cheese mixture, then cover with another layer of pastry or filo, sealing the edges. Make slits in the top to allow steam to escape, and brush with egg or milk. Sesame seeds can be also scattered over the crust before baking.

Bake at 180° C/gas mark 4 for around 30 min, until the pastry is golden brown. Serve hot or cold.

Ingredients (for 4 people)
500 g fresh spinach
150 g onions and/or spring onions, chopped
1 large leek, washed and chopped (optional)
2 garlic cloves, crushed
200 g *féta* cheese
1.5 tsp dried dill or 2 tbsp fresh, chopped
1.5 tsp dried parsley or 2 tbsp fresh, flat-leaved, chopped
75 ml olive oil
salt & pepper

For the pastry
400 g filo *or* 450 g puff *or* 425 g shortcrust

recipes

eat

Yemistá me kimá (Stuffed peppers and tomatoes)

Peppers, large tomatoes, large courgettes and aubergines can all be stuffed with the rice and meat or rice stuffing. A very popular lunchtime dish — but very filling. For this

recipe allow one stuffed vegetable per person as a starter, two or three for a main meal. For a vegetarian version, omit the mince *(kimá)* and double the rice.

Cut off the tops of the peppers and tomatoes and set aside. Hollow out the insides. Chop and save the tomato pulp. (If preferred, the whole peppers can be blanched in boiling water for around 3 min, then drained well and cooled before filling.)

Brown the mince and soften the onion in some of the olive oil, add the tomato pulp, garlic (if used), rice, half the parsley, and salt & pepper. Simmer for around 8 min, until the liquid is absorbed. Check that the rice doesn't stick, and add extra tomato juice or stock if needed. Add the pine nuts and raisins (if used). Mix well together, spoon into the hollow tomatoes and peppers and replace the tops.

Ingredients (for 4 people)
6 tomatoes
4 red peppers
500 g lean minced meat
125 g short grain rice
1 onion
2 garlic cloves, crushed (optional)
500 ml passata or 1 x 400 g
   tin chopped tomatoes (sieved)
100 ml olive oil
3 tbsp fresh parsley, chopped
50 g pine nuts (optional)
50 g raisins (optional)
1/2 tsp cumin (optional)
salt & pepper
breadcrumbs (optional)

Note: Cooked left-over rice can be used in *yemistá*. After browning the mince, etc, add the other ingredients and cooked rice. Simmer until the excess moisture is driven off, then use to stuff the vegetables.

Pack the stuffed vegetables firmly in a greased dish or roasting tin. Pour over the remaining olive oil and tomato juice. Sprinkle over the breadcrumbs (if used). Cover the dish tightly with foil and bake for about 45 min at 180° C/gas mark 4. Remove the foil and bake a further 10 min.

Variations: The same filling can be used to make *papoutsákia* (stuffed aubergines and courgettes; literally 'little shoes'). Cut the courgettes lengthwise or aubergines in half. Scoop out the pulp and save to cook with the filling. Brush some lemon juice in the empty cases to prevent them discolouring. A large tin of chopped tomatoes replaces the tomatoes in the main recipe. Top with béchamel sauce (made with 1 heaped tbsp of flour, 25 g butter, 200 ml milk, 1 small egg and a pinch of ground nutmeg). After filling the vegetable cases with the cooked mixture, spoon over the sauce and sprinkle with grated cheese. Place in a shallow tray or dish and bake, uncovered, at 180° C/gas mark 4 for 30-40 min.

Tzatzíki (Yoghurt dip) *not illustrated*

The ubiquitous accompaniment to most Greek meals. There is often a raised eyebrow if this isn't part of your order but, of course, it's not to everyone's taste.

Squeeze as much liquid out of the cucumber as possible and mix well with the yoghurt. Add the garlic to taste (you may not want it too strong), a touch of olive oil, a little salt & pepper, and dill if used. Garnish with olives to serve. Taste as you go!

Ingredients (for 4 people)
250 g strained yoghurt (see shopping tips, page 31)
1 small cucumber, coarsely grated
2-3 garlic cloves, crushed (or sometimes finely grated)
olive oil
salt & pepper
fresh dill, chopped (optional)
fresh olives (garnish)

Not many people visiting Greece on a casual basis find the Greek language easy to get to grips with. The first obstacle is the Greek alphabet itself. It uses a fair number of characters not represented in the Latin alphabet. In many situations, particularly with place names, road signs and even menus, it is deemed important to change the Greek over to the Latin alphabet to make the names more understandable to foreigners. Unfortunately, there is no definitive or official way to change Greek letters to their Latin equivalent for some of the reasons outlined below. This itself just adds to the confusion, as you will see.

Learning one or two of the pitfalls shown here should help with reading menus in tavernas and with some pronunciations.

The trouble with 'g': On the face of it, this seems a fairly straightforward transliteration. The problem is that 'g' is pronounced as 'y' when preceding 'i' or 'e', but as 'g' in other instances. So a word like *gemistá* (meaning 'stuffed', as in tomatoes or peppers}, is often written as *yemistá* — the way it is pronounced. *Ágios,* meaning 'saint', is another common word regularly mispronounced by visitors. Again the 'g' has a 'y' sound, so it sounds like *áyios.*

The trouble with 'mp': Since the letter 'b' is pronounced as a 'v', it leaves the alphabet without a 'b' sound. To overcome this, a combination of letters, 'mp' is used. This combination is pronounced as 'b' at the start of a word, but as 'mb' anywhere else in the word. The Greek word *mpampou* is a classic illustration. That is how it might be written as a conversion from the Greek alphabet — or equally, it could be written *bambou.* From here it is only a small step to recognise it as 'bamboo'. The mp/mb confusion is commonly noticed on the menu with

GREEK

lamb chops, often seen as 'lamp' chops — which raises a smile with visitors (… but the Greeks would pronounce it as 'lamb' anyway).

'Lamp' cutlets

The trouble with 'nt': This is another combination of letters which is pronounced as a normal 'd' at the beginning of a word and 'nd' elsewhere. It crops up in words like *ntomátes* (tomatoes), which can also appear as *domátes*. This combination is used when a hard 'd' is required, because the 'd' in the Greek alphabet is pronounced as a soft 'd', almost like a 'th'. The word for two, *deo*, for example, is pronounced *theo*.

There are one or two other letter combinations with special pronunciations, but those above are the ones most commonly encountered and the most useful ones to learn.

In the menu and shopping listings, we have used the transliteration that points the way towards the correct pronunciation, but remember that the stress (´) is important too!

CONVERSION TABLES

Weights		Volume		Oven temperatures		
						gas
10 g	1/2 oz	15 ml	1 tbsp	°C	°F	mark
25 g	1 oz	55 ml	2 fl oz			
50 g	2 oz	75 ml	3 fl oz	140°C	275°F	1
110 g	4 oz	150 ml	1/4 pt	150°C	300°F	2
200 g	7 oz	275 ml	1/2 pt	170°C	325°F	3
350 g	12 oz	570 ml	1 pt	180°C	350°F	4
450 g	1 lb	1 l	1-3/4 pt	190°C	375°F	5
700 g	1 lb 8 oz	1.5 l	2-1/2 pt	200°C	400°F	6
900 g	2 lb			220°C	425°F	7
1.35 g	3 lb			230°C	430°F	8
				240°C	475°F	9

MENU ITEMS

aláti salt

angoúri cucumber

arakás peas

arní lamb

 kokkinistó in tomoto sauce

 kléftiko in filo parcel with veg/ cheese

 lemonáto in herb sauce with lemon

brizóles chops

psitó roast

áspro white

áspro krasí white wine

astakós lobster

atherina small, whitebait-like fish

axionó sea urchin

bakaliáros cod

baklavá filo pastry, nuts soaked in syrup

bámies okra, ladies fingers

barboúni fish similar to red mullet

biftékia mince done as a beefburger

bira beer

bouzákia grilled lamb or goat

briám similar to ratatouille

brizóla chop

deípno dinner

dolmádes vine leaves, rolled and stuffed with mince and rice

domátes tomatoes

 yemistés stuffed with rice, herbs and maybe mince

elaiólado olive oil

eliés olives

Ellinikós kafés Greek coffee (never with milk)

 glykós sweet

 métrios medium sweet

 skétos plain, simple (no sugar)

fasolákia green beans

fáva yellow pea purée

féta feta cheese

 saganáki sto foúrno oven-baked feta with tomatoes and peppers

filéto filet

fráoules strawberries

fréska froúta fresh fruit

galaktoboúreko filo/ custard sweet

galopoúla turkey

galéos cod

 me skordaliá with garlic dip

garídes prawns (pronounced garithes)

g(y)emistá stuffed

g(y)iaoúrti yoghurt

 me méli with honey

g(y)ígantes giant butter beans in sauce

giouvétsi veal in a clay pot with *manéstra*

glyka dessert ('sweet')

g(y)úros meat from large skewer

haloúmi cheese

halvás sesame/ sugar sweet

hoirinó pork

hoiriní brizóla pork chop

horiátiki saláta Greek salad

hortofágos vegetarian

hoúmous hummus

imám baíldi stuffed aubergine

kafés coffee

 frappé iced

me gála with milk

kakáo hot chocolate

kakaviá fish soup

kalamári squid

karídes walnuts

karpoúzi watermelon

kataífi pastry, like shredded wheat strands, soaked in syrup

katálogos menu

 krasión wine list

katsíki goat

kávoures boiled crab

kimá mince

keftédes fried meatballs

kléftiko see *arní kléftiko*

kolokithákia courgettes

 tiganitá fried

kolokithokeftédes fried courgette balls

kokkinistó veal in tomato sauce

kokteil cocktail

kondosoúvli spiced port on a spit

koniák cognac

kotolétes cutlets

GLOSSARY

kotópoulo chicken
koukiá broad beans
kounéli rabbit
krasí wine
  áspro or lefkó
  white
  kókkino red
  rozé rosé
krokétes croquettes
kserotígana (thíples)
  deep-friend
  pastry
ksifías swordfish
ksúdi vinegar (pro-
  nounced kseethi)
ládi oil
lákano cabbage
loukániko sausage
loukoumádes
  honey-soaked
  batter balls
makaróni spaghetti
  me kimá bolog-
  naise ('with
  mince')
manéstra rice-like
  pasta
manitária mush-
  rooms
marídes small fish
  (like whitebait)
maroúli lettuce
melekoúni see
  pastéli
méli honey
melitzána aubergine
melitzánosaláta
  aubergine dip
mesimerianó lunch
mezédes starters
  (mezés for short)

míla apples
moskári beef or
  veal
mousakás moussaka
múdia mussels
neró water
nes instant coffee
oktapódi octopus
omeléta omelette
orektiká first course,
  starters
oúzo aniseed spirit
pagákia ice (cubes)
pagotó ice cream
païdákia lamb
  chops
papoutsákia half
  aubergines
  stuffed with
  mince, tomato &
  onions, with a
  cheese topping
pásta cake, pastry
pastéli sesame and
  honey bars
pastítsio baked
  meat and pasta
  dish
patátes potatoes
  (often synony-
  mous with chips in
  tavernas)
  tiganités chips (full
  description)
patzária beetroot
  cooked with its
  leaves
pepóni melon
pipéri pepper
piperiés peppers
yemistés stuffed

with rice and
  meat
pita pita bread
pitaroúdia Rhodian-
  style chickpea
  patties
pítsa pizza
portokáli oranges
proinó breakfast
psári fish
psarotavérna fish
  taverna
psetó roast
psomí bread
retsína resinated
  wine
revithia chickpeas
revithokeftédes fried
  chickpea balls
rígani oregano
rúzi rice (pro-
  nounced reezee)
rúzogalo rice
  pudding
saganáki fried
  cheese starter
saláta salad
saligária snails
  yiáxni in a casse-
  role with tomato
  sauce
sándouitz sandwich
sardéles sardines
seftaliá home-made
  sausage
sikóti liver
sikotariá fried liver
  and kidney
simiakó small sweet
  shrimps from Sími
skordaliá garlic/

mashed potato
  dip
skórdo garlic
soúpa soup
soutzoukákia spicy
  meat rolls
souvláki meat on
  skewer
spanakópita spinach
  pie in filo
spetzofáï sausage
  and peppers in
  spicy sauce
stafúlia grapes
ste soúvla spit roast
stifádo meat stew
  with shallots
sto foúrno baked in
  the oven
strídia oysters
talagoútes small
  thick (sweet)
  pancakes
taramosaláta fish
  roe paste dip
thalasiná seafood
tiganitá/és/ó (all
  variations mean
  'fried')
tirí cheese
tirokeftédes cheese
  balls
tirópita cheese pie
tirosaláta spicy
  cheese dip
tónnos tuna
tost toast
tsáï tea
tzatzíki yoghurt,
  garlic, cucumber
  dip

vradinó evening
  meal
vrastó boiled
yaoúrti yoghurt
yemistá/és/ó (all
  variations mean
  'stuffed')
youvétsi veal stew
  with *manéstra*
zambon ham
zákari sugar
zesté sokoláta hot
  chocolate

SHOPPING TERMS

allspice *bakári*
  (whole or ground)
apples *méla*
apricot *veríkoko*
aubergine *melitzána*
bananas *banánes*
basil *vasilikós*
bay leaf *dáfne*
beans, french
  fasolákia
beans, broad
  koukiá
beef *moskári*
beer *bíra*
bread *psomí*
bread (olive) *elioté*
butter *voútero*
cabbage *lákano*
cake *pásta*
carrots *karóta*
cheese *tirí*
cherries *kerásia*
chestnut *kastaniá*
chicken *kotópoulo*
chickpeas *revíthia*

chocolate *kakáo*
chop *brizóla*
cinnamon *kanéla*
coffee *kafé*
  instant *nes*
courgettes
  kolokithákia
cream *kréma*
cucumber *angoúri*
cutlets *kotolétes*
dips
  aubergine *melitzá-
  nosaláta*
  fish roe paste *tara-
  mosaláta*
  garlic/mashed
  potato *skordaliá*
  spicy cheese *tiro-
  saláta*
  yoghurt/garlic/
  cucumber *tzatzíki*
eggs *avgá*
feta cheese *féta*
filet *filéto*
fish *psári*
  cod, dried *baka-
  liáros*
  cod, fresh *galéos*
  sword *ksifías*
  tuna *tónnos*
  whitebait-type
  marídes
flour *alévri*
fresh *fréska*
frozen *katepsig-
  méno*
fruit *froúta*
garlic *skórdo*
grapes *stafélia*
ham *zambón*
honey *méli*

ice
  cubes *pagákia*
  cream *pagotó*
lamb *arní*
lettuce *maroúli*
liver *sikóti*
margarine
  margaríni
meat *kréas*
  on a skewer, for
  barbecuing
  souvláki
melon (water)
  karpoúzi
melon *pepóni*
milk *gála*
mince *kimás*
mushrooms
  manitária
mussels *múdia*
octopus *oktapódi*
oil *ládi*
  olive *elaiólado*
olives *eliés*
onions *kremédia*
oranges *portokáli*
oregano *rígani*
oysters *strídia*
parsley *maïdanós*
pastry *pastá*
peach *rodákino*
peas *arakás*
pepper *pipéri*
peppers *piperiés*
pork *hoirinó*
potatoes *patátes*
prawns or shrimps
  garídes
rabbit *kounéli*
rice *piláfi*
rosemary *dendro-*

lívano
salad *saláta*
salt *aláti*
sardines *sardélles*
sausage *loukániko*
  home-made
  seftaliá
seafood *thalasiná*
shrimps (small,
  sweet, from Sími)
  simiakó
snails *saligária*
soup *soúpa*
spaghetti *makarónia*
spinach *spanáki*
squid *kalamária*
sugar *zákari*
strawberries
  fráoules
tea *tsaï*
tomatoes *domátes*
turkey *galopoúla*
veal *moskári*
vinegar *ksúdi*
  (pronounced
  kseethi)
walnuts *karídes*
  (pronounced
  kareethi)
water *neró*
wine *krasí*
  white *áspero krasí*
  red *kókkino krasí*
  rosé *rozé krasí*
yoghurt *yiaoúrti*
general
bottle *boukáli*
kilo *kiló*
half-kilo *misó kiló*
carrier bag *sakoúla*

bold type: photograph; *italic type: map*

INDEX

Second edition © 2013
Published by Sunflower Books
PO Box 36061, London SW7 3WS
www.sunflowerbooks.co.uk

ISBN 978-1-85691-434-5

The authors especially thank Maria Thymianou of the Greek National Tourist
  Office in Rhodes Town and Stefanos Karasiotos of the Rhodian Beach Hotel
Cover photograph: Commercial Harbour, with the Marine Gate in the
  background (Walk 2)
Photographs: Brian and Eileen Anderson
Maps: Sunflower Books, adapted from Road Edition and old military maps
Series design: Jocelyn Lucas
Cookery editor: Marina Bayliss
A CIP catalogue record for this book is available from the British Library.
Printed and bound in China by WKT Company Ltd

Before you go ...
log on to
www.sunflowerbooks.co.uk
and click on '**updates**', to see if we have been notified of any changes to
the routes or restaurants.

When you return ...
do let us know if any routes have changed because of road-building, storm
damage or the like. Have any of our restaurants closed — or any new ones
opened on the route of the walk? (Not Rhodes Town restaurants, please; these
books are not intended to be complete restaurant guides!)
Send your comments to mail@sunflowerbooks.co.uk